StoryFrames

Helping Silent Children to Communicate across Cultures and Languages

Cynthia Pelman

Grosvenor House
Publishing Limited

All rights reserved
Copyright © Cynthia Pelman, 2023

The right of Cynthia Pelman to be identified as the author of this work has been asserted in accordance with Section 78 of the Copyright, Designs and Patents Act 1988

The book cover is copyright to Cynthia Pelman

This book is published by
Grosvenor House Publishing Ltd
Link House
140 The Broadway, Tolworth, Surrey, KT6 7HT.
www.grosvenorhousepublishing.co.uk

This book is sold subject to the conditions that it shall not, by way of trade or otherwise, be lent, resold, hired out or otherwise circulated without the author's or publisher's prior consent in any form of binding or cover other than that in which it is published and without a similar condition including this condition being imposed on the subsequent purchaser.

A CIP record for this book
is available from the British Library

ISBN 978-1-80381-623-4
eBook ISBN 978-1-80381-625-8

Cynthia Pelman

Cynthia Pelman M.A., M.Sc.
Speech and Language Therapist
2023

Registered member, Royal College of Speech and Language Therapy UK (RCSLT)
Registered member, Health and Care Professions Council, UK (HCPC)

This book is dedicated to two once-silent children
who were willing to tell me their stories.

In this book I use the pronouns they/them to refer to children in general, and the pronouns she/her and he/him to refer to two specific children who participated in the research programme.

***

TABLE OF CONTENTS

Introduction	A brief history of the StoryFrames programme	ix
Chapter 1	The 'Silent Period'	1
Chapter 2	To intervene or not to intervene?	13
Chapter 3	Ways to intervene	21
Chapter 4	The StoryFrames programme	28
Chapter 5	Setting up the StoryFrames programme	40
Chapter 6	Implementing the StoryFrames programme	50
Chapter 7	S is for Safe Secluded Space	52
Chapter 8	F is for Feelings	54
Chapter 9	R is for Repeating	58
Chapter 10	A is for Adding	61
Chapter 11	M is for Modelling	67
Chapter 12	E is for Expanding	75
Chapter 13	A showcase of achievement	85
Chapter 14	A window onto an inner world	92
Chapter 15	Measuring change	97
Chapter 16	Endings	103
Bibliography	Sources used as reference in this book	105
Appendix I	Quick Reference: A summary of the StoryFrames programme	113
Appendix II	Language assessments used in the original research project	114
Appendix III	The development of language and communication skills	119
Appendix IV	Expanding high-level conversations	122
Appendix V	The miniature hand-made books of the Bronte family	125
Author biography	Cynthia Pelman biography	127

INTRODUCTION

A brief history of the StoryFrames programme

The StoryFrames programme was originally developed as part of the requirements for a Master's degree at the University of London (Teaching English as a Second Language) in 2009 in England.

The research for the programme was carried out in a kindergarten with two children, one (Child A) aged 4 years 6 months and the other (Child B) aged 3 years and 8 months. These two children had not spoken at all at school since arriving in the class, even though they were able to talk at home, in their home language.

The children both spoke a language other than English in their homes: Child A spoke German and Child B spoke French. Their families had recently relocated to the United Kingdom. Their parents reported that at home they were verbal and sociable, and played with other children who spoke the same language. If they went out shopping or to a playground with their parents they would speak freely to the family. At school, however, these two children were completely silent.

They did not greet anyone on arriving and did not reply when a teacher spoke to them. They were usually seen standing on the sidelines, watching the other children but not interacting with them, and would play alone when the other children were playing together.

Colette Granger (2004) provides the background to our attempt to understand these children and their silence. She suggests that it is not so much the difficulties involved in the acquisition of the new language, but rather the losses which the child experiences in the move to a new country, which seem to lead to this kind of silence. Not only is their own language not spoken or understood, but the very way in which they have always interacted with other people is no longer the norm. The familiar places and faces are no longer present.

Granger suggests that for these children, "... the traumatic event ... is the loss of the self that dwelled in the first language." Another researcher in this field talks of the loss of "a feeling of belonging and of participation in the community" (Toohey and Norton 2001).

This book attempts to describe and to understand what it might feel like to be one of these silent children, and how we might be able to support them at school.

A story about how this experience might feel was related to me recently (personal communication) by someone, now an adult, who was ten years old when they arrived in the United Kingdom. This child knew no English, but knew it would be necessary to learn this new language and was happy to do so. The child had however no idea that the English alphabet might be different from the alphabet of their home language.

When the child first saw the English script being written on the blackboard, they were amazed, and presumed that the teacher had developed some kind of impressive hieroglyphics for the lesson. The child looked around at the class to see the faces of the other students, wondering why they too were not looking amused, or amazed.

We see from this example how even one's most basic assumptions, as to what is strange or funny or unusual, might not fit in with the culture in which one finds oneself. This child suddenly understood that even one's sense of humour needs to be adjusted, or re-created.

This same child was not able to talk to or understand anyone in the school, and therefore memorised a short sentence: "My name is...." and simply produced this sentence every time anyone spoke to them. This then became cause for amusement on the part of the other children in the class, and the new child could not grasp why that would be funny, thinking that being able to say one's name in a new language must surely be an accomplishment.

The effect of this kind of experience on a child, both cognitively and emotionally, is not to be underestimated.

The research programme which led to the StoryFrames Programme

The two children who took part in the research programme on which StoryFrames is based were at a kindergarten I was visiting regularly in my role as speech and language therapist, in order to provide teacher training related to the needs of children with speech or language difficulties. The teachers asked me to see these two children, about whom they were very concerned. Child A had been attending the kindergarten for 18 months, for two days each week. Child B had been attending for 8 months, every day.

The children were offered two half-hour sessions of therapy per week, spread over the duration of one school term (six weeks). Due to timetabling issues and public holidays, Child A participated in a total of eight sessions, and Child B had ten sessions.

In this short time both children made significant gains in three important areas: they become more socially interactive with their peers; they became more confident in their ability to speak to their teachers, and their level of English, as measured for both vocabulary and grammar, developed by an average equivalent of six months in only six weeks.

I witnessed Child B, after the programme had ended, using language assertively in role-play in the classroom: he was playing the role of a teacher, using a confident and fluent voice, telling other children, who were playing the role of students, what they should be doing. This was a very different child from the one observed a few weeks previously, sitting very still and not responding when the teacher called his name for the register.

Child A was, by the end of the programme, talking to other children, joining in their games, and using a wide range of social language functions in talking to her teachers: making requests, answering questions, saying hello and goodbye. Her teacher told me that before the programme nobody in the school had ever heard her voice, and now "I hear her voice everywhere!"

The StoryFrames programme was thus found to be a brief, effective and low-cost way of promoting communication skills in these children who were new to the country, new to the language being spoken in their school, and who were totally silent at school, all day and every day, for several months.

***

In introducing the programme, it is also important to say what this programme is *not.* It is not a programme to teach English as a second language. Rather, it is a programme to support the child who, for any of a multitude of possible reasons, has become silent and socially isolated when at school, while remaining fully verbal and communicative in their home, in their home language, and with people familiar to them.

The StoryFrames programme does not need to be carried out by a speech and language therapist. Using this manual, a teacher, teaching assistant or social worker can easily learn to use this programme. In this book I will be referring regularly to "the teacher" but this could equally be anyone who is concerned and involved, and who has some background in working with young children.

The theory behind the programme is presented in depth, and there are clear instructions as to how to carry out the different steps of the programme. The equipment consists only of low-cost and easily available toys and books.

As a programme which aims to support the silent child to move towards social interaction, it is the *quality of the interaction* between the teacher running the programme and the silent child which is at the core of the work, and which is the main factor in the success of the programme. Of course, social interaction is largely carried out through the use of language, and during this programme we not only use language, but also support the child in the development of their use of language, but this is not the primary focus.

Since this original research project with children in the Silent Period, I have used the method with many children in my general speech and language therapy practice. These are children with a wide range of communication difficulties: developmental language delay or disability, children who stutter, shy and retiring children, and children on the autistic spectrum.

I have found the programme to be very helpful with these children, who have difficulty expressing their ideas, wishes and concerns. They may then tend to fall silent because they lack the confidence to speak, knowing they might be misunderstood. Sometimes listeners do not have the time or patience to wait while the child struggles to produce words and sentences. The StoryFrames method has been helpful in giving these children positive experiences in using the language they have, however halting, to express themselves. The step-by-step and stress-free nature of the programme allows the children to experiment with talking, in a safe space, and to gradually build up their confidence. This programme can therefore be a useful adjunct to other teaching or language therapy programmes for children with speech or language difficulties, although this was not the initial purpose of the programme.

The programme as described in its entirety below is tailored specifically for the child at pre-school or kindergarten, or in the early years of education, who is new to the country, new to the culture and the language of the country, and who is going through the 'Silent Period' at school.

The programme can be presented in any language. It is the way the teacher interacts with the child, and not the language which is being spoken wherever these children may find themselves, which is the core of the programme, and which makes the StoryFrames programme so effective.

***

CHAPTER 1

The 'Silent Period'

The StoryFrames programme is designed to support children who are struggling with two simultaneous challenges.

The first challenge is for those children who do not know the language being spoken at their school. These children would be likely to experience significant difficulty in socialising with other children, as well as difficulty in participating in classroom learning activities. This group might include refugees, children from migrant families, or children in families that have simply relocated from a different country.

The second challenge is that some children, new to a school, do not speak at all, and they may remain completely silent at school even after having been exposed to the new language for a long period of time. These may be children who are, by temperament, unusually shy or reticent. They can sometimes be described as Highly Sensitive Children (Aron 2002). They may have undergone traumatic experiences during their re-location from their home country. They may simply be overwhelmed by the number of recent changes in their lives: losing their previous homes, and the people they once knew, and coming to a new place with a different climate, a different way of life and a different language.

The StoryFrames programme was tailored for children who fall into both of the above groups simultaneously. Moving away from their home country and familiar environment can result in their feeling shy, confused, and unsure of the social norms in the new place. Add to this the trauma of re-location, the emotional hurdle of not knowing the language being spoken around them, not understanding instructions, and not being able to ask for anything they need, and it is easy to surmise why such a child might remain silent.

This silence, which can last for many months, is referred to in linguistic and educational research as the 'Silent Period'.

***

Does the Silent Period really exist?

The Silent Period is a phenomenon which is sometimes encountered when children attend a school where the language of instruction and of social interaction is different from their home language. Krashen (1981) describes this as a characteristic and even necessary part of the process of second language learning in children: the silence is part of the process of learning the new language, and does not mean that the child is not listening. During the Silent Period, according to Krashen, the child is absorbing the new language and achieving a level of understanding of this language, after which the child will be ready to begin speaking.

The Silent Period is so variable in degree and duration that it is difficult to come to any general conclusions. Some children learning a second language hardly undergo a silent period at all; they use non-verbal communication to socialise with other children, and very quickly begin to pick up the new language. Others are silent in some circumstances and not in others; they may talk to one specific child, or may respond if a teacher asks them a question, even if they may not yet initiate conversation. Some overcome the Silent Period in a few weeks or months, and others do not. Most researchers agree that it is not possible to set an average duration for this Silent Period, as the variability is so large, with many other factors coming into play as possible causal factors, and possible maintaining factors.

There is indeed some debate as to whether there is any validity at all in the concept of the Silent Period. For example, Roberts (2014) suggests that there is limited evidence of such a period occurring, and that some of the research studies have used inconsistent criteria. Different studies define the Silent Period in different ways. In addition, there are various types of simple classroom support techniques which have been found to be effective in helping these children to overcome their initial difficulties in a short time.

Saville-Troike (1998) presents evidence that the Silent Period is actually never completely silent, and that many of these children do sometimes engage in "private speech"; they may start to use the new language but in a non-communicative way, for example, repeating a phrase or word that someone else has said, or privately rehearsing something that they might wish to say.

It may be helpful to view the silence of these children as being positioned on a spectrum of silence. Some do indeed begin speaking and interacting with teachers and children at school in a very short time. Some, who fall in the middle of the spectrum of silence, may be silent most of the time, for a few months, but if spoken to gently, by a sympathetic teacher or child, they may reply using short sentences or one-word answers. Other children, at the other extreme edge of the spectrum of silence, remain completely silent for many months, and do not interact with or play with other children at all.

The research dealing with the Silent Period appears to fall into different groups, according to the academic discipline of the researchers: linguistic, socio-cultural and psychological.

The linguistic view

In the 'linguistic' explanations, the reasons for the child's silence are considered to be basic to the process of learning the new language (Krashen 1981). In these theories, it is suggested that the child is actively processing the second language as 'input' and that silence is a necessary and normal stage before the child can begin to speak the language. In such theories, the silent period is sometimes called the 'pre-production' period, on the assumption that it is a normal, necessary and time-limited stage towards learning a second language.

The theory proposes that learners of any language (whether learning their home language or learning a second language, and whether they are children or adults) need first to focus on extensive listening and comprehension (i.e. input) before they can produce output (spoken language). According to this explanation, the child will, in time, pick up enough language simply through being exposed to the language, and will start to communicate. It is, after all, well-known that young children can learn two, three or even four languages, simply through adequate exposure, something which adults find much more difficult (Byers-Heinlein and Lew-Williams 2013). There has been much discussion in the research about the "critical period" for language learning; generally there is consensus that the younger the child begins exposure to the new language, the better (Byers-Heinlein and Lew-Williams 2013). There seems to be general agreement that a child of preschool or early school age is usually able to learn a second or even a third language using the same emotional and cognitive mechanisms involved in learning a first language.

Taking the purely linguistic input position (that all the child needs is sufficient exposure to and interaction in the new language) has led some researchers (for example, Clarke 1997) to the conclusion that the Silent Period is a normal and temporary process which the child should overcome in time without any additional support. This kind of theory is often referred to as a 'wait and see' theory. If after some time the Silent Period does not end, then it can be dealt with later.

This position has been confirmed to a significant extent by recent research about "language usage" (Tomasello 2003, 2019). What Tomasello adds to the discussion, however, is the idea that it is not just the exposure to language which matters, but the fact that the exposure occurs in a very specific kind of context - a context of meaningful and interactive communication, in which the adult speaker holds a conscious intention to make the language comprehensible to the child. It is this which is the essential precursor to language learning, whether the child is acquiring their first language, or learning a second language.

A slightly different explanation for the silence of the child learning a second language is that of Parke and Drury (2001) who postulate that the exposure to a language different from the home language causes "an interruption in the process of normal development of language" in the young child; such an interruption could be the result of replacing one language with another, or adding one language system to another already acquired, and thereby imposing a heavy cognitive load on the child.

It is important to keep in mind another aspect of linguistic development: that a bilingual child may have a co-occurring speech and language delay or disability, which is unconnected with their second language status. Distinguishing whether this is the case can be a matter of some difficulty. If such a child has an intrinsic language difficulty such as Developmental Language Disorder (DLD) this would affect the development of both their home language and the second language (McGregor 2020).

Developmental Language Disorder is a significant, developmental and on-going difficulty in understanding and/or speaking in the child's home language. DLD was previously known as Specific Language Impairment (SLI). There is no known cause of DLD; it is not caused by emotional difficulties or by limited exposure to language. DLD is also not caused by other conditions such as hearing loss, physical impairment, Autism, severe learning difficulties, or brain injury (McGregor 2020).

Tests of comprehension and of expressive language in the child's home language, as well as careful observation of the child in their home setting, would therefore be important in providing a precise picture of the silent child's language development in their home language.

However it is often difficult to find the resources to carry out a full speech and language assessment for every child at a school. In addition, it is sometimes difficult to find a competent speaker of the child's home language who is able to do such an assessment, and as a result some children with DLD might not be identified early. In such a case, I suggest that participation in the StoryFrames programme might serve as a diagnostic tool in deciding which children to refer on to speech and language therapy. Those who make good progress in this programme would possibly not require further intervention.

If it is found that there is indeed a significant delay in the child's home language, then speech and language therapy would be indicated. The StoryFrames programme described in this book might then be used as part of that therapeutic programme, but would not be sufficient in itself to address the difficulties of such a child.

The socio-cultural view

Socio-cultural theories take a wider view than the solely linguistic view, and see the child as at all times existing in a world of interaction with other people. Learning is seen as a mostly social, and not individual, process; development results from interaction with the people close to the child. In these views, language is an aspect of social interaction and not something which exists as an isolated modular skill.

The socio-cultural position emerges from the work of Vygotsky (1986), Lave and Wenger (1991), Wenger (1998) and Rogoff (2003). This approach brings to the fore issues about social participation and integration, and around 'making meaning' within a social space. In this view there is no separating the language being spoken from the person in the society, or from the culture in which that language is being used. Language is not something to be learned in isolation from social interaction and then used for social interaction; rather, language is one aspect of social interaction.

Wenger talks of the child attending a new school in a new language as needing to "construct [an] identity" in relation to the community they are newly entering. It is not so much a matter of learning the language as of learning to participate in this new social world. Such learning requires the child to repeatedly "negotiate meaning" in this new culture (Lave and Wenger 1991), to accept and in time adopt social practices that are initially new and unknown, and to gradually overcome the strangeness of this new world and learn to live as a social member of the new culture.

Another socio-cultural aspect to consider is that cultures can differ widely from one another in relation to their attitudes to silence. Some ethnographic studies (for example, Yamamoto and Li 2011) highlight the vastly differing attitudes to quietness, and to behaviours which are retiring and less verbal, in non-Western societies as compared to Western societies. Those who come from a culture where children are not encouraged to be verbally outgoing are more likely to be classified, when attending a school in the West, as shy or socially avoidant, while in fact they are simply acting according to the social norms for children in their own culture.

In traditional families in China and Japan, children who are quiet and retiring are seen in a positive light, as being sensitive to the needs of others, and acting politely and respectfully towards their teachers and elders. Attentive listening is preferred to vocal assertiveness.

Chen et al (1992) describe the outcomes of comparative research carried out in China and in Canada. It was found that in these countries, the kinds of children who were seen by others as desirable playmates were very different. In China, those children who were seen as more desirable were quiet and almost unassertive, while in Canada, the most desired playmates were those who were outgoing, talkative, and gregarious.

In some cultures, it is considered rude for a child to make eye contact with an adult. In some African cultures, one's name is considered sacred and symbolic, and people are not addressed by their formal name; such a child would be alarmed and upset if a teacher called them by their formal name.

The way people greet each other in African and Asian countries is often completely different from the greeting norms in Western countries. There may be different types of greetings for different places, times of day, times of religious festivals, and for people of different ages and social status. There may be rules about who initiates the greeting: often the child or the person of lower social status has to be the person to make the opening greeting. The specific forms of greeting may differ according to kinship and occupational roles. In some countries it is considered impolite to talk during meal times. Different cultures also have a wide range of social norms for gender-appropriate behaviour (Tannen and Saville-Troike 1985).

Non-verbal behaviours in the act of greeting are also socially prescribed: the distance at which one stands from another person, whether one offers a handshake, whether one is required to sit down while greeting an elder (Omar 1991; Ntuli 2012; Sommer and Lapapula 2012; Ameka and Breedveld 2004).

We see therefore that different cultures attach different meanings to speech as well as to silence. As a result, the adjustment of such children when moving to a Western country might be very difficult, and the vast amount of social learning which needs to take place in order to cope with apparently simple everyday tasks such as greeting must be daunting for a newcomer. The kind of support such a child might benefit from would need to carefully and respectfully take into account these aspects of their home culture.

This is not to suggest that cultural attitudes discouraging children's assertiveness do not appear in the West too. In some schools in Western countries, children are still required to be "seen and not heard" and to engage in minimal verbal classroom participation (Shaik 2015) in order to maintain classroom discipline and to adhere to norms regarding the rights of children when in the presence of adults.

In some cases, such attitudes are applied more stringently to girls than to boys (Houston and Kramarae 1991, Doey et al 2014) although attitudes have changed somewhat since their earlier research of 1991. These attitudes might play a part in the silence of young girls at school; Houston and Kramarae talk about some of the ways in which women are silenced in the wider society, such as family hierarchy 'rules', and lack of representation in politics and in the media. The high levels of domestic violence should also be mentioned here, in connection with the hierarchies of power in society and the silencing of abused women and children.

When we think from a social-psychological point of view about what language is and what language does, it is important to remember that language is not simply a skill that we either have or do not have; it is also one of the main ways in which we relate to other people. If we are not able to speak the language which the people around us are speaking, we are limited in the ways we can relate to them, and they to us.

This is possibly one of the primary factors in the silence of these children: they can no longer relate to others through language, as there are not likely to be children in the new country who speak their language; and they have not yet learned a new way.

In some cases, especially with immigrant families (Arizpe et al 2014) there may be pressure put on the child to avoid using their first language, and to speak only in the language of the new country. This is sometimes the case when the immigrant family is going through arduous bureaucratic processes of trying to be granted leave to remain in the new country.

The silence of the child might therefore be the only possible choice they have. Granger (2004) puts it well in describing such a child: "With the door to expressibility in the first language closed behind her, and confronted with a not-quite-open door in the second language, she must simply do the best she can."

The psychological approach: Intrinsic personality traits linked to silence

A different point of view seen in the research is one which looks at the silent period as linked to traits such as shyness and introversion, that is, as something intrinsic to a child's individual personality. A very comprehensive summary of current thinking about shyness can be found in an article by Scott (2006).

There is no denying that many children are able to easily enter into a new language-culture and to find their place socially. They begin to participate actively and to learn the new language remarkably quickly. There is a vast difference between the child who does not know the language of their peers but has the type of temperament which enables them to use gesture, to join in the play of other children, and to actively participate in school activities, as opposed to the silent child who stands on the edge of the group, who watches but does not join in, and who is too shy to ask to go to the toilet.

Why is it then that some children in this situation remain silent, for weeks or months, and do not adapt? In these 'personality' theories, shyness is defined as "a temperamental trait characterized by a fear of novel social situations and self-consciousness in situations of perceived social evaluation" (Doey et al 2014). Shyness includes "over-concern with social evaluation ...[which] leads to the shy person inhibiting social contact, withdrawing, and avoiding social situations" (Zimbardo 1977).

In the case of such a temperament, a child who is not fluent in the new language might be so concerned about failing to express themselves correctly that they fall silent rather than risk such failure.

There has been extensive psychological and developmental research into issues relating to children who are shy or retiring. Shyness has been associated with negative responses from others towards the child, such as exclusion or victimisation in peer relationships (Sugimura 2018). Shyness has also been linked to other problematic aspects such as anxiety and poor outcomes at school, as well as poor outcomes in both cognitive and social aspects in later years (Cordier et al 2021, Prior et al 2000).

Similarly, Gardner and MacIntyre (1993) describe some children who have "language anxiety" which is "the propensity for an individual to react in a nervous manner when speaking.... in the second language" (p 5).

Granger describes the possibility of a deeper underlying fear around the use of this new language: the silence is "symptomatic of a kind of fear not of *making* but rather... of *being* a mistake" (Granger 2004) [own italics].

Kagan (1989) similarly approaches the issue of the silent period from an individual child's point of view: he suggests that these children might be temperamentally "inhibited", and will present in general (not only in the school setting) as cautious, retiring, and retreating from social interaction. This kind of temperament will then affect them significantly at school, where they might not only be fearful of making a mistake in the way they speak, but also reluctant to draw attention to themselves in any way. For these reasons, Kagan suggests, these children will take much longer than average to emerge from the Silent Period.

What could be the aetiology of such shyness? Evolutionary theories suggest that once humans began living in bigger groups, hierarchies of power developed, and shyness or introversion or just 'taking a back seat' was one way to manage these social pressures. For example, William James (1890) following Darwin and taking an evolutionary view, viewed shyness as a basic human instinct with a self-protective function in relation to power hierarchies in prehistoric societies, in which case this is an adaptive feature of evolution, and is simply a reflection of the wide variety in human personality.

We need also to take into account the possibility of the child having experienced a high level of trauma if, as refugees, they have experienced the shock of displacement, danger, and fear (Dangmann et al 2022; Arizpe et al 2014). In such a case, the silence can be a reaction to the fear and uncertainty surrounding these experiences.

Any family re-locating to a new country and a new culture will have gone through some stress and anxiety. Parents having to re-make their lives, perhaps searching for new employment opportunities, and themselves feeling that everything around them is new and strange, will certainly find that their stress is felt, and shared, by their child.

Ellis et al (2006) refers to "condition sensitivity". This is a response of extreme sensitivity on the part of some children to developmental experience, to changes and to discontinuity. The child with such sensitivity will perceive new situations as more threatening than a child with a more resilient personality. Kagan (1989) refers to the sensitivity of some children to any change in routine, or anything new and unusual in their environment. He uses the term "neophobia" for the fear of anything new or novel in their circumstances, and describes the dread such a child might feel for anything unanticipated or previously not encountered. A child who is highly sensitive to novelty, and who has moved to a new country, whether due to the family's choice or as a result of traumatic circumstances, is surrounded by an entirely new and unanticipated environment, and as a result may respond with shock, possibly accompanied by silence.

The traits of introversion, shyness, social anxiety and social phobia are differentiated in the research and have been documented extensively, although there is often much overlap in these diagnoses. There is also a wide spectrum of severity for each, with Selective Mutism generally considered to be a subtype of social phobia (Hoffman and DiBartolo 2014). In daily health and educational practice, however, it seems that the differentiation is not as precise (Peterson 2019, Brown 2022). In psychological theories and in the therapy professions, the borders between shyness, extreme shyness and social anxiety or phobia have often become blurred.

A very simplistic distinction holds that social anxiety and social phobia are similar, and include a fear of a wide range of social situations. For the silent child at school, who usually only has difficulties at school, and only when faced with the need to communicate in the new language, but does not show any difficulties at home and with their wider family, a diagnosis of social anxiety or social phobia may be less likely; their problem seems to be specific to the school setting and language.

It is useful to add to the discussion the concepts of shame and embarrassment. Lewis, in his extensive investigation into the emotion of shame (Lewis 1995) tracks the earliest evidence of embarrassment in children at age 2-3 years. Reddy (2008) would place this even earlier in the child's life. These concepts are useful in gaining a wider understanding of the child's experience of the Silent Period. Whether or not the silent child is by nature, or by temperament, shy or anxious, there might certainly be cause for a feeling of embarrassment and shame when a child, who was previously able to make their ideas, thoughts and feelings known through language, is now suddenly prevented from doing so.

An important concept in the research into children's behaviour is that of the "Highly Sensitive Child" (Aron 2002). This is the child who typically responds with extreme sensitivity to changes in the environment, to noise, to over-stimulation, and to anxiety in themselves and in their family. This trait of high sensitivity can lead to a wide range of behaviours, influencing how the child interacts when in a large group, or with people who are unfamiliar. Aron points out that "They may refuse for a few minutes, hours, days or even months to speak to adults, strangers, or in class" (Aron 2002 p 11).

Boyce (2019) recommends, for such sensitive children, that the family try to maintain predictable day-to-day routines to prevent the sensitive child from responding adversely. Boyce suggests that it is not vulnerability, but rather a heightened sensitivity to the circumstances around them, that defines the Highly Sensitive child.

Aron's research has found that as many as 20% of a population might be described as Highly Sensitive: this is not a disorder to be treated, but rather just one aspect of the wide range of personalities we might find in any classroom.

If therefore we take a wider view of the recent experiences of the silent child, new to the country and to the language, we can factor in a combination of stresses: their parents are themselves suffering from stress and anxiety; the child is placed for several hours a day in a school where not only is everything unfamiliar, but their parents are unavailable to talk to and to protect them; and even the home language which the young child has so recently acquired is no longer of any use. We can then see a crushing combination of stresses on the child - a kind of 'perfect storm' - where the number of unfavourable circumstances is simply too much to cope with. And so the child becomes silent. It is perhaps more a matter of being silenced, than of choosing to be silent.

A useful way to see this silent period is through the psycho-analytic approach of Colette Granger, who views the silence as "a message in itself", and attempts to understand what meaning the silence holds for a particular child. She suggests that traumatic loss of identity may accompany the loss of a first language, and proposes that the silence of the student learning a second language may signify a process not so much of moving from one language to another as "from one self to another" (Granger 2004).

This approach, which parallels the words of Winnicott (2018) who talks about "the right not to communicate", is based on the conviction that the child who is being silent is not just unable to communicate in the new language, but is also making a choice and expressing their sense of agency in deciding not, at this stage, to try to talk.

A similar view is presented by Hoffman (2008) who writes about the trauma of feeling that her entire self was a different self in the country of her childhood, and that she needed to discover, or create, a new self in order to live in the country they had moved to.

Other writers see the issues around shyness as explained by the very fundamentally human "need to belong" (Baumeister and Leary 1995). The child who is both new to the school and new to the language may feel that they lack a sense of such belonging, that they are outsiders and do not have the right or the option to join in.

In response to these issues, the StoryFrames programme is designed to promote in the child a sense of attachment and belonging - in this case, attachment to one specific teacher at the school. In the programme, the teacher running the programme provides the child with consistent and responsive interpersonal attachment, situated within the school premises. This in some way can satisfy the child's need to belong, as the teacher becomes an agent of safety in the school space and a bridge towards communication with a wider range of people.

An integrated view of the silent period

The issue of the Silent Period is thus not a simple one. Taking into account the variety of theories and the wide range of presenting behaviours and outcomes, we see that this is not an issue where one explanation will suffice.

The various explanations presented above emerge from different theoretical backgrounds: linguistic, cognitive, social, anthropological and emotional. However, the very tendency to divide the issue of the Silent Period into separate academic disciplines tends to hide the real issues at stake for the child. Gregory (2002) speaks of rejecting these categories, and accepting that the issue "transcends disciplines, as it focuses on the inextricable link between culture and cognition through engagement in activities, tasks or events."

Similarly, Spence and Rapee (2016) in their analysis of social anxiety disorder, take a wider view, and see these difficulties as a result of a complex combination of several possible causative factors: the impact of genetic and biological influences, cognitive factors, emotional and temperamental factors, peer relationships, parenting, adverse life events and cultural variables. Although their research is about social anxiety disorder in general (and not specifically in relation to the Silent Period) they point to the importance of one factor which some silent children have experienced: recent negative life events in the child's personal experience, and the impact of these on the child's ability and desire to interact socially.

The work of Danon-Boileau (2001) with silent children provides considerable insight into their specific needs, and suggests ways to intervene sensitively and successfully. Danon-Boileau (2001 p 3) suggests three main likely causes for the silence: cognitive reasons (a cognitive or perceptual delay or disability); a speech and language disability, and what he terms the "symbolic group": those children whose difficulties appear to be more emotional than cognitive. In working with these children, one of these causal factors might carry more weight than another, but all of them need to be taken into account.

The language acquisition theory of Tomasello (2003) describes the complex array of emotional, social and cognitive skills which operate simultaneously in the acquisition of a child's first (or 'home') language. These co-occurring factors would apply equally to a young child learning a second language.

In the StoryFrames programme we take into account the wider context of the child's own life (Drury 2007, Bligh 2011). In the case of a refugee or migrant child, this would include trying to gain an awareness of when and why the child moved from their home country to a new country, how easy or traumatic the move had been, and whether there are significant cultural differences between the original country and the new country.

In the case of the child immigrant, there are additional factors to take into account. Such a child might well be feeling terrified at the experience of the transition to the new country (Arizpe et al 2014) and there might be continuing stresses on the family regarding the bureaucratic processes involved in obtaining residence in the new country. The ongoing fear of not being allowed to remain permanently, and of perhaps having to move on to another place at some time, must play a part in the emotional stresses on the child. In such a case, learning the new language may seem rather pointless, as a quite different new language might soon be needed.

It is also important, if possible, to include in our consideration any personal or familial events which might have impacted on the child's feelings of security and continuity, before, during and after the move. A child in whose life there have been sudden and extreme changes (bereavement or divorce) may also respond with silence at school, due to their difficulty in facing such changes with resilience.

It is this complex interplay between the intrinsic personality, the socio-cultural variables and the life story of each child which might lead to one child remaining in the Silent Period for many months, while another is able to adapt socially and communicatively in a short period of time.

In summary, there are perhaps five main causes for a child's silence at school, and the presence of any or all of these five, and the interactions between them, are the factors most likely to lead to a child being silent at school. The five factors are

- Forced second language learning
- Extreme changes in the life circumstances of the child (such as refugee or migrant status, re-location from another country, or bereavement or divorce)
- Differing cultural attitudes towards speech and silence
- Social anxiety, social phobia and Selective Mutism
- Intrinsic personality traits or temperament

Having this personal, historical and cultural information does not, in itself, change how the StoryFrames programme is run. However, an awareness of the child's individual history, as far as is possible, goes a long way to help the teacher running the programme to be sensitive to important issues in the child's life, and to act accordingly.

The StoryFrames programme was created in an attempt to take all of these factors into consideration, but at the same time to be simple enough to use with any child, without specific training, and with a minimum of equipment and basic techniques, so that in spite of the multiple complexities the child might be facing, some useful support can be provided within the school space by a teacher.

Please note however that the StoryFrames programme is not, and could never be, a strategy to overcome a diagnosed social phobia or social anxiety, or significant trauma. If you are at all concerned that the child's mental health is compromised, please contact the Child Mental Health services in your area.

***

Selective Mutism

It is important to note here that the shy or retiring child, who is new to a school and to the language being used there, is different from a child with Selective Mutism. Selective Mutism is usually seen as a social phobia, specifically regarding speaking in public places, or in any place outside the home. It can present in children who are not faced with learning a second language.

It is sometimes difficult to distinguish between the silent child who is shy or Highly Sensitive, and the silent child who has a social phobia which is being expressed as Selective Mutism. In general, the child with Selective Mutism shows very rigid boundaries between where they will and will not speak; even if they do speak at home to their families, they will not speak to their families in the presence of other people. The child in the Silent Period often does speak to their family when the family pick them up from school, even if there are other people around.

The child with Selective Mutism might also show their intense anxiety in their posture and movement, and in progressively adding to the number of places and people with whom they will not speak. The child in the Silent Period, on the other hand, will remain relatively relaxed in the classroom setting, even though they do not speak, and will usually retain a consistent, and not worsening, level of silence.

If you are in any way unsure as to whether a child has Selective Mutism, please do not delay, as for children with this difficulty a very specific Speech and Language programme is advised, and early intervention is crucial to prevent the situation from becoming entrenched and exacerbated.

Please consult a speech and language therapist if you are concerned. Useful information is available on the SMIRA website http://www.selectivemutism.org.uk/

***

CHAPTER 2

To intervene or not to intervene?

When a teacher has a silent child in the classroom, a decision is required: whether or not to provide a specific, individualised programme of support for this child. If we do decide to intervene, there are multiple ways of doing so.

Deciding which path to take usually involves consultation with school staff, the Special Needs Coordinator at the school, and the child's parents. Of course, issues around staffing at schools, and budgets for extra intervention, are always an important consideration, but there are many other factors which must be considered in this debate. I present here some of these factors which need to be taken into account in deciding whether or not to intervene, as well as some typical types of intervention being used in classrooms.

- **Negative stereotyping of ordinary shyness**

In considering whether or not to intervene, we must also consider whether we are unfairly judging the silent child to be in some way falling below what is required and expected at school. Is this just a normally shy or moderately introverted child?

Much of the research being presented in this book has been carried out in the USA, the United Kingdom and Australia: that is, in Western countries. This matters, because there is a prevailing attitude in Western countries that views shyness as a negative character trait. This attitude could lead to the inequitable pathologising of a child who is naturally quiet and socially retiring. Aho (2010) warns that research carried out in America will be likely to provide a distorted view of the kind of child we are thinking about: he suggests that the American view not only penalises shyness, introversion, and "modesty and humility", but also actively values and promotes extraverted behaviour. This tendency then views shyness as belonging to the category of emotions to be abolished.

Several researchers have focused on this "negative stereotyping of ordinary shyness" (Hoy 1993). Scott (2006) refers to this issue as "the medicalisation of shyness". Craib (1994) proposes that there exists in modern Western society an idea of a perfect human, devoid of all negative emotions, who will never undergo any unpleasant social experiences. He suggests that this idea is misguided, and describes it as a Western myth that serves to support the "omnipotent status" that we have accorded to the various psychological therapies. Craib shows how Western societies have a strong tendency to try, through the various kinds of psychological therapies, to eradicate the tendency of humans towards any negative emotions at all; Freud (1895) refers to this as "normal human misery" or "ordinary unhappiness" – that is, a part of normal life, and not something which needs to be 'fixed'.

With such negative attitudes towards shyness, we are perhaps implying that the child is failing "to achieve certain cultural values, such as assertiveness, self-expression and loquacious vocality" and we are making a judgement that "…. shyness is …a problem for which people can, and should, be treated." (Scott 2006). Such an attitude might lead us to intervene in ways which might not be helpful or appropriate, or even necessary.

An alternative view is to see shyness not as an intrinsic failure or dysfunction, but as just one of many types of behaviour on a spectrum of traits, ranging from introversion to extraversion. In this case we may be more reluctant to intervene; our responsibility then becomes one of determining where on the spectrum of silence the child's difficulties might lie, and to make careful decisions as to whether or not, or to what extent, that child needs additional support at school.

Another important issue to be aware of when considering the silent child is our own expectations of gender differences: shyness may be less socially acceptable for boys than for girls because "it violates gender norms related to male social assertion and dominance" (Doey et al 2014, Houston and Kramarae 1991).

As teachers, parents and therapists, we do want the children we work with to feel happy, to have friends and to communicate. For Craib (1994), Granger (2004) and other writers, these feelings of empathy should not be allowed to stop us from allowing that the child has a right to their response to the events in their life. We need, in Craib's words, "… to respect [their] symptoms, where others refuse[d] to allow it; to respect [their] suffering as a choice which might, in context, be [their] best choice." As Winnicott (2018) says, a child has a right to be silent, and a right not to communicate.

- **Fluctuating social situations in the classroom**

It is important not to assume that the context for the child in the classroom stays the same while we are deciding whether or not to intervene. Any changes in the social situation in the classroom during the school year need to be carefully monitored.

For example, if a new teacher takes over, or if a friend or sibling of the silent child has been off sick for a while, the situation may feel very different for the silent child.

This was relevant to the experience of one of the two children in the original StoryFrames programme. When Child B started school he entered a class which already had several very confident and articulate children; child B was at that stage completely silent both with teachers and peers, as well as being socially isolated. After a few months, when some of the dominant older children left the kindergarten to go up to the next year group of school, he started joining in the play of other children, even though he was not yet speaking to them. Such changes in the dynamics of a class may provide the silent child with a way to move forward.

- **Identification with one's first language**

An aspect which is important to consider and respect is the extent to which the learner's identity is bound up in their first language. Having to learn and use a new language might lead to the feeling that their identity is being changed or eroded by contact with the additional language and its culture (Hoffman 2008). Krashen uses the term "Affective Filter" (Krashen 1981) to describe the anxiety, low motivation and negative attitudes of a child towards the second language itself, which can act to prevent a student from learning a second language.

The feeling of reluctance to give up one's first language is expressed clearly in Hoffman's writing (2008). She describes how she felt not only confused and unable to express her wishes in the new language, but she also felt as if she had become a different person since she left her home country, a person she herself did not recognise. She expresses the belief that our thinking is carried out in our internal language, and the absence of this internal language represents a loss of the ability to think.

The close link between cognition and language is an issue which appears in the 'Sapir – Whorf' hypothesis (after the two linguists who debated this issue many years ago.) The theory proposes that different languages impose on the speaker different kinds of thinking categories. The result is that speakers of different languages 'see' the world differently, based on the language they use to describe the world. These thinking categories or patterns therefore both reflect and retain the culture which speaks that language.

An example is the way in which different concepts of time are reflected in French and in English. English uses just one word for the concept of 'time' reflecting three different meanings: the 'time' of day, the 'time' it takes to do something, and how many 'times' we have done something in the past. In French, there are different words for each of these three concepts (heure, temps, and fois). On the other hand, the French word for 'weather' is the same word, 'temps', which is also used to express how many times we have done something (Hofstadter and Sander 2013). Such conceptual differences are significant when learning a second language and may be adding to the difficulties of the child.

There is another important aspect of how languages function as much more than just the transfer of information from one person to another. Specific words and phrases in one's home language "conjure up a host of social and cultural attitudes, beliefs, memories, and emotions" (Gleitman and Papafragou 2005). The effect on the child of having to learn not only new words and grammar but also new social norms and new conceptual patterns of meaning must be taken into account.

The challenge of learning a second language is therefore much broader than a matter of acquiring vocabulary and syntax. If it is the case that the home language 'carries' the child's emerging cognitive system, as well as treasured cultural values and memories, then the debate about whether or not to intervene must include creative ways to celebrate and maintain the child's own language and culture, and in some way to help the child recognise that this has not been lost, and can still be retained and valued, even when entering a new language and a new culture. In the event of a child being discouraged from using their home language, and this does occur sometimes (Arizpe et al 2014) the loss must be even greater, as the home language is now presented as something to be rejected.

If we accept that language is an inextricable part of a culture, we must then also accept that language is an inextricable part of the identity of the speaker of that language. This means that an extra layer of difficulty exists in becoming bilingual: it is not just a matter of adopting a new language, and adopting or adapting to the culture of that language (Cummins 1981) but of perhaps adopting a new identity as well. As Hunter (1997) puts it, the second-language learner might need to adopt "multiple, shifting and conflicting" identities, as opposed to the perhaps unitary identity of the native speaker of a single language. This can place a heavy burden on the child.

Social, cultural and temperamental considerations

We have already discussed (see Chapter 1, socio-cultural theories) the ways in which different cultures view silence differently. It is important to take into account the life context and culture of each child, and to consider that the child might live in a culture which might have very different social norms from the norms of the school (Yamamoto and Li 2011).

In addition, rather than automatically seeing shyness as a fixed and perhaps undesirable personality trait, intrinsic to the child, we need to take into account individual differences and preferences in the personality and temperament of each child. The silence might be a normal and even adaptive response to a very different social environment. We should not rush to intervene without careful consideration.

In summary, the decision to provide specific and individualised support for a child who is not talking at school is not to be taken lightly. We must remain aware that intervention is not simply a matter of helping the child to learn the new language, but of taking into account the wider context of this child's life, and the possible underlying wish to remain fluent in their own original language, as a way to retain and value their original cultural identity.

For these reasons, schools should always build strong links with the child's family: the school needs to share information about the child with the family, and also to gather information from the family about the child's home culture. The school and the family should work together in supporting the child (Brooker 2002). When the silent child is from a culture where talking freely to adults outside the home is discouraged (as may be the case especially for girls in certain cultures) we need to respect the child's need for silence as a value, and provide time and support to enable the child to learn not only the new language but a new way of being outside the home.

"The principle of acceleration"

Having presented several reasons to be cautious before intervening in the silent period, there are, on the other hand, several very convincing factors which do promote the provision of support for the silent child. These are educational theories which recommend, as a matter of principle, intervention for any child who is struggling in any way at school.

The theories fall under the general heading of a "principle of acceleration" (Alexander 2004). These theories take the position that what is required for a child to learn any new skill, whether social or cognitive, is the carefully-considered and conscious decision to actively provide the support that the child needs. 'Wait and see' is not an option.

Feuerstein (2015) uses the term "mediation" in the same vein, although in a broader sense. He refers to the way all adults in any culture mediate the world to the children of that culture, and in this way enable children to learn all aspects of the culture in which they are growing up:

the language, the values, and the cognitive skills needed to function at school and to survive and thrive in the world. The non-provision of this mediation places the child in a condition of social, cognitive and emotional deprivation. In this sense, intervention is what schools are for, and a decision not to intervene, and not to provide support for the silent child, is not acceptable.

Feuerstein's ideas about mediation parallel the socio-cultural position of Vygotsky (1986): the way a culture is transmitted from one generation to the next is not to assume that the child will pick up what needs to be learned simply from observation and from experiencing life in that culture, but rather as a result of the deliberate, intentional, planned and careful mediation, by adults, of all aspects of that culture to the child.

This mediation is carried out by the people accomplished in the skills of that culture. This includes all life skills, such as weaving, building, cooking and writing, but also talking, conversing, and living a socially connected life in accordance with the social norms of that culture. Without this mediation, these skills and knowledge of the culture would not be adequately transmitted. For Feuerstein, and other theorists of the principle of acceleration, any event or situation which might prevent any child from accessing such mediation is an indication that intervention is not only advisable, but ethically required.

The principle of acceleration clearly applies to the silent child. As with all other aspects of the acquisition of a culture by a young child, the first language, or 'home' language, is learned through the child being immersed in consistently intentional interactions with adult caregivers. It is the combination of context and language, and the intention to share those with the child, which enables a child to link the sounds of words and phrases to the meaning of what is going on around them. To withhold this from the silent child is to assume that the child will learn a second language by simply being in the presence of a new culture, and by being exposed to the language through listening. To hold such an expectation of a child is to demand something which we do not expect from a child learning their first language.

The "output hypothesis" in second language learning

This hypothesis is the result of research carried out by Swain (Swain 2001, Swain and Lapkin 2002) who found that in learning a second language, the actual experience of speaking out loud to other people is an essential ingredient. Children who are merely exposed to extensive input do not acquire facility in speaking.

This will of course have significant implications for the silent child who is reluctant to speak to others, whether due to shyness, or to unfamiliarity with the language, or both. Such a child will be exposed to the second language, and will hear it daily, gaining extensive input, but will not get to experience output, that is, the experience of actually speaking, which Swain and others propose as being so vital in the second language learning process. In such a case, intervention is crucial, even if only as a way to provide the child with sufficient opportunities to experience speaking aloud to another person. There is sufficient evidence to accept that the silent child learning a second language will need to have *both* intensive input *and* output opportunities.

In summary, when trying to make a decision as to whether or not to intervene with the silent child, these "usage-based" theories (Tomasello 2003) provide strong motivation for intervention. The StoryFrames method has been developed with this in mind.

Language as a necessary catalyst for cognitive development

Another factor in favour of providing support for the silent child is to ensure that their cognitive development is not adversely affected by their not understanding the language being spoken in the classroom.

Preschool and school are spaces in which extensive cognitive development take place. Whether the school ethos is free play, or guided play as in some preschool teaching methods, or formal academic teaching, the time that children spend in the early years of education is crucial for the development of the basic cognitive skills which they will need during their entire school career. School is not just a matter of learning facts, but of *learning how to learn*: school develops in the child cognitive skills such as sustained attention, analytic thought, categorisation and comparison, and logical cause and effect (Feuerstein and Fallik 2015). These cognitive skills depend heavily on language. A child who does not have sufficient language to follow a school lesson will be heavily disadvantaged. The decision not to intervene will then have consequences for the child's cognitive development and subsequent academic success.

There is much debate as to the direction of connection between language and thought. Katherine Nelson (1996) describes language as a "catalyst for cognitive change". There is strong evidence in the research which shows a cyclic effect: language helps us to develop abstract concepts and higher order thinking, and in turn, this high-level thinking helps us develop more complex language (Gleitman and Papafragou 2016). Language is used "in organizing and channelling thought that is already mentally present." (Gleitman and Papafragou 2016).

Certainly this is the case for abstract and philosophical concepts, such as 'justice', or 'tolerance'. Feuerstein (2015) shows how language is required in order to be able to think about these superordinate concepts and to move beyond the concrete vocabulary of everyday naming. The lack of such concepts in the new language would severely limit the child's ability to think abstractly and inferentially, to process information and to make decisions which involve abstract thought.

It is vital therefore that the child who does not understand or use the language of instruction in the classroom is provided with support to ensure that the cognitive concepts being developed in the classroom are mediated to this child.

The social and emotional effects of isolation on the silent child

One of the most important factors in favour of intervention is the effect of the Silent Period on the emotional well-being of the silent child.

The question which needs to be asked is this: while we do need to think about what causes such a child to be silent, we are also obliged to consider the effects of this silence on the child. We need to be aware of what the silence does to the child, and we need to be clear that there is much more at stake than the issue of learning a second language.

It is only once we consider these issues carefully that we can make relevant decisions about intervention.

The problem is expressed beautifully and clearly by the poet Rabindranath Tagore (1985).

STORYFRAMES

> "The singer alone does not make a song,
> There has to be someone who hears."

The writing of Bakhtin, the Russian philosopher (1981) and literary critic, emphasises how we all exist in a social world. Communication is seen by Bakhtin not as something a person does individually, in order to send a message to a receiver (in the way that we might send a text message) but rather as an interaction between two people. Bakhtin describes how a person only begins to exist fully if they are the "subject of an address", that is, if their existence is confirmed by the existence of others who are communicating with them, who are relating back to them, in a mutual interconnection. Bakhtin also uses the term "an answering consciousness": the knowledge that when we communicate, there is someone there to respond. It is this which provides both a motivation to interact and the feedback to continue our interaction with other people.

Similarly, the philosopher William James (1890) writes how a person who is not in a communicative relationship with others must suffer unbearably at being ignored, at not being noticed: the result of this must be that such a person feels that they are not being recognised as a person who exists.

The problem is not only that the child does not initiate contact or answer if someone speaks to them. The silence itself becomes a factor which cuts the child off from engagement with others: the less socially 'inviting' or approachable the child seems, the less likely it is that other children will want to initiate social interaction with them.

Silence and shyness have been found to be linked to being bullied or victimised by other children (Sugimura 2018). The silent child's social isolation can lead to long-term detrimental consequences in self-esteem and the ability to forge friendships.

Children who are not verbal become therefore ever more socially isolated, having few opportunities to join in activities or play unless their peers and their teachers actively invite and encourage them. In the words of Vasuvedi Reddy (2008 p. 27) such a child is prevented from sharing in the kind of direct engagement in which another person acts to "call out from [the child] a different way of being, an immediate responsiveness, a feeling in response, and an obligation to 'answer' the person's acts".

The experience of being silenced, due to no longer being able to express oneself in one's first language, and thus not being able to express even one's basic needs, must in itself lead to some emotional trauma (Hoffman 2008). Hoffman writes movingly about the loss of identity she felt when moving to a different country: the self she had been, and the self she was familiar with and comfortable with, had to be reconstructed in the new language and in the mores of the new country. The process was lengthy and traumatic for Hoffman.

On an emotional level, being linguistically and socially competent in the language spoken by teachers and peers promotes a feeling of belonging and of participation in the community (Toohey and Norton 2001). The lack of this would be likely to lead to a feeling of being excluded from the community, and could have lasting negative effects on the emotional well-being of the silent child.

Children also use their communication skills to learn to negotiate peer conflicts and discover socially accepted ways of initiating and participating in peer play (DaSilva and McCafferty 2007). The child without language would have no opportunity to learn how to manage such peer interactions.

A factor which is often forgotten when working with the silent child is that this child is very different from children who are learning a second language, but who have in their class other children who they can speak to, and who are also learning the second language. In such a case, these children are all in the same social learning situation, are all able to communicate with each other, and continue to do so even while learning a second language. Much of the research on children learning a second language takes place with children who are in a classroom with other children who are also learning the second language, and who, outside of this classroom, do have a language in common with each other.

We are here talking about a very different situation. The silent child is usually the only child in the class who cannot speak to the others at all. The silent child is learning a second language not due to their family wishing to provide them with educational and cultural enrichment, but rather due to their having to survive in a new and unfamiliar country. Add to this the possibility of traumatic experiences in their relocation history and we have a clear reason to consider these children as being in need of additional support which goes beyond the usual second-language acquisition theories.

For all the reasons listed above, it becomes clear that it is difficult to justify non-intervention using a 'wait and see' attitude. We are obliged to consider the effect of the isolation on a child who continues to attend school, day after day, without being included in play or in learning.

A good general approach in deciding whether to intervene would be to observe the child for several days, at different times of the school day, as well as in different school spaces (in the classroom, in the playground, at lunch) and to consult with the child's parents and class teacher, before making any decisions.

There are no hard and fast rules about quantifying the level of silence which should arouse our concern, but the term "spectrum of silence" is useful in classifying the level of the child's silence in terms of its position on a scale between two extreme points. A child who is interactive and participates in most aspects of the school day, even if the child does not yet speak the new language, would be at one end of the spectrum. A child who may speak only in certain circumstances, with a very small number of people, but who will respond non-verbally when spoken to, might be mid-way on the spectrum. A child at the worrying end of the spectrum would be one who fulfils most or all of the following criteria:

- Not responding to greetings (hello and goodbye)
- Not replying when their name is called on the morning register
- Not asking the teacher for anything during the day
- Not singing along with familiar songs
- Not playing with other children in the 'pretend play' corner of the classroom
- Consistently seen at the edge of a group of children, watching but not joining in
- Not playing with other children in the playground

The concept of silence falling along a spectrum thus enables us to find some sort of measure, however qualitative, of the child's silence, and to determine the level and urgency of need for intervention. The term "spectrum of silence" is also useful in explaining the child's difficulties to parents or teachers.

***

CHAPTER 3

Ways to intervene

Once we have analysed where on the spectrum of silence the child might be positioned, and have decided accordingly that intervention is required, we need to make a number of decisions: What kind of intervention is most suitable? What should the duration of the intervention be? Are there adequate economic and staffing resources for such an intervention? This chapter describes various published and well-researched options to consider.

General classroom intervention methods

An approach to the Silent Period often taken by schools is not to intervene with individual therapy programmes, but rather to use a range of classroom teaching strategies to support the child.

Making extensive use of visual cues such as gesture, facial expression, mime and pictures while teaching can be very effective. Asking the child to draw what they are trying to say is another useful visual technique.

It is sometimes helpful to ask the child to teach the teacher words in their own language, or to draw pictures of their family and the country they lived in previously.

Arranging activities which include the repetition of words or phrases, or counting repeatedly, and in general exposing the child to lots of spoken language, even if the child does not respond, is also helpful.

In order to ensure that the child does not miss out on important learning material, some schools include after-school lessons with a small number of children, revising the material covered during the day. Some schools provide the child's parents with notes and advice so that they can assist with homework.

A classroom-based strategy which focuses on the child's social position in the classroom might involve setting up a 'buddy system' with a sociable child who will include the silent child in their games.

All of these are valuable tools in the teacher's daily practice. However, these techniques can only be successful when the child is willing to communicate, but is being held back purely by the lack of language. These techniques usually do not work in the case of children who are on the extreme end of the spectrum of silence, as these children might not be willing or able to respond non-verbally, and might come to feel that the amount of attention being given them is overwhelming. With some silent children, even if we are acting with the best of intentions, trying to chat with the child, and encouraging the child to join in, often results in anxious retreat on the part of the child.

A different kind of approach is clearly needed.

Intervention through making changes in the classroom social ethos

The exclusion of people who look or sound different from the majority is unfortunately seen at times in any social group. The acceptance of difference by society plays a vital part in enabling a new child to integrate into school life.

Toohey and Norton (2001) argue from a social interactionist point of view that the factors which make a child a confident participant in a classroom are not only the child's own inner resources (cognitive, emotional and social) but also the extent to which the other children are prepared to accept the incomer as a participant in their play and social activities.

The kind of intervention which might be needed would then focus on the social attitudes of other children towards the silent child. Interventions implemented to change such attitudes would need to cover issues around responses to outsiders, to difference, and to newcomers in general, and the intervention would ideally need to be provided to all the children and staff in the school.

However, social change of this kind is usually very gradual. This kind of intervention would of course be beneficial in the school over the long term, but may not be sufficient to support the silent child in the short term.

Intervention through adjustment of teaching techniques and teacher-child relationships

The issue of the relationship between teacher and child is also to be considered and could be a factor in the decision as to how best to support a specific child.

One study looked at the frequency of teacher-child interactions in the classroom and found that some shy children might be at risk of not being able to form positive relationships with their teachers, thus perpetuating the likelihood of the child remaining silent in the classroom (Rudasill and Rimm-Kaufman 2009). In this case, intervention might comprise advice to school staff, and perhaps not include direct intervention with the silent child.

Teaching technique adjustments might also be needed when working with other children who have been marginalised or silenced. For example, responses towards disabled children on the part of teachers might include fear of disruption in the classroom, feelings of being burdened by additional educational needs, and unconscious attitudes towards disabled bodies which could lead to reduced social interactions between teachers and children (Symeonidou and Loizou 2023).

It is easy to understand why a teacher might feel uncomfortable with silence as a response from a child. Teachers are primarily responsible for helping children to respond to what they are teaching. We may sometimes feel that if, in spite of all our efforts, there is no response, perhaps we are not doing something we could have been doing.

There is also the issue of institutional or governmental curriculum demands. Teachers are obliged to regularly measure the progress of their students using specific assessments, and these assessments are, in early years' education, often based on evidence of children's active and vocal participation and responses in the classroom. There is therefore a burden on teachers to show evidence that the children they teach are learning, and to do this, they need the children to be speaking. It can be helpful therefore for teachers to have an awareness of the psychological and socio-cultural views on the Silent Period, in order to defend the position they are taking with regard to the children in their classrooms.

Children with autism, who may present with behaviours which are not the norm in a classroom, are also at risk of being marginalised. In such a case, perhaps unconsciously and without any intended malice on the part of teachers, the child may not be included fully in the kind of reciprocal communication that other children benefit from.

I have already mentioned children with speech and language delay or disability. Their language difficulties can lead to their social isolation, and if compounded with their need to learn a new language, they might become even more marginalised than they would have been in other circumstances. Similarly, a child who has a stutter, or whose speech is slow and effortful (dyspraxia or dysarthria) might become the target of negative responses and sometimes even victimisation from other children and even from teachers. At the very least, listeners may not allocate the amount of time such a child requires in order to complete what they are trying to say, and these factors will in effect silence all but the most determined children.

In the research about methods of teaching, there are two very different metaphors used to describe different concepts of teaching and learning: one in which the individual needs to acquire knowledge which the teacher provides (sometimes called the "acquisition" metaphor on the part of the learner, or the "transmission" metaphor for the role of the teacher) and the other view, in which the learner is "encultured" into a community, sometimes called the "participation" metaphor (Sfard 1998, Wenger and Nuckles 2013). Changes in teaching style in this regard may play a large part in alleviating the difficulties for the silent child. Tabors (2008) provides extensive advice on good practice for classroom work with children who are acquiring a second language.

Usage-based theories of language acquisition in young children

Usage-based theories of language learning (Tomasello 2003) focus on both input and output of language, in very specific interactional contexts. The basis of Tomasello's theory is that humans are, by their evolutionary nature, motivated to infer the needs of others, and to see the communicative acts of others as being relevant and meaningful (Sperber and Wilson 1995, Tomasello 2003, 2019).

Humans act cooperatively to achieve this by sharing attention and sharing intention. We use joint attention to read others' intentions (sometimes called mind-reading, or inter-subjectivity). Joint attention occurs when both the child and another person are paying attention to the same object or event, and are also, at the same time, acknowledging that they are both doing this (Tomasello 2003, 2019). In this way, a young child starts to share experiences and connect with the minds of others.

Tomasello points out that in addition to this basic attitude of attention and intention, language learning depends on the cognitive skills of pattern recognition. These are the basic cognitive skills which enable the child to parse the flow of the sounds of language and to find patterns through which to infer meaning. It is through recognising repeated patterns of sound and reference that the child begins to make sense of the words and phrases they hear.

Children thus begin to comprehend words and phrases as carrying symbolic meaning, because these words and phrases appear in a context of shared meaning, and of a shared intention to communicate meaningfully. This theory is therefore simultaneously social, cognitive and linguistic. In these theories, "language structure emerges from language use" (Ghalebi and Sadighi 2015).

In making a decision whether or not to intervene with the silent child, we cannot assume that the kind of language context which the child experiences on any normal day in the classroom will be such as that described by Tomasello. The classroom teacher usually has at least 25 other children to attend to, and cannot be expected to provide the kind of intensive interactional communicative experience which a child might experience at home learning their first language, and which the silent child might need in order to be able to move beyond silence.

For this reason, a small-group or one-to-one programme might be necessary for these children. Even taking into account the fact that the silent child is already an effective communicator in their home language, that is, that they do already have the required cognitive skills of joint attention and pattern recognition needed to learn a second language, their time in the classroom simply cannot supply the intensive interpersonal and interactional context which is needed for learning a second language.

Of course, teachers cannot adjust their teaching techniques to suit the needs of a single child, when all the other children in the class are dependent on the teacher to use teaching techniques which are helpful to them. However, the published second language programmes described below do provide some helpful techniques which can be adopted and can benefit the entire class.

A few of the well-known and successful programmes, based largely on usage-based theories of language learning, are described below. Of course this is far from a definitive list; the choice is vast. These few examples show how most of these programmes, while very effective for most second language learners, do not take into account the very specific needs of the silent child. In working with the silent child we need to always keep in mind the complex interplay of factors involved in their silence: socio-cultural, linguistic and emotional.

The programmes described below are 'The Natural Approach', 'Total Physical Response', and 'Teaching Proficiency through Reading and Storytelling' (TPRS.)

'The Natural Approach'

One of the teaching methods developed in accordance with Krashen's 'input' theory is the Natural Approach (Krashen and Terrel 1983).

Terrel adapted the input theory somewhat: input is intensively used, but extensive output is in fact also expected. This method (unlike those input programmes which work on providing exposure to natural conversation only) includes explicit grammar and vocabulary exercises. The Natural Approach also uses music and games, puzzles and problem-solving activities, which necessitate considerable output.

In spite of the use of explicit grammatical and vocabulary exercises, the stated focus in the 'Natural Approach' is on enabling students to communicate their thoughts and ideas, and to communicate responsively, whether they are using grammar correctly or not. The emphasis is on content and use of language, rather than on form, in the belief that language learning is subconscious, and not achieved through conscious grammatical practice.

This method also applies Krashen's "affective filter hypothesis" (Krashen 1981) which states that anxiety around learning prevents learning. The inclusion of music and games provides a relaxed, enjoyable atmosphere which can reduce anxiety and promote learning.

The silent child might indeed benefit from such a stress-free atmosphere. If such a programme were provided in small groups, or even one-to-one with the silent child, it might be effective. However there remains the concern that the method assumes that the learner will actively and verbally participate in the interactions and games; this is of course the very issue with which the silent child has such difficulty.

For this reason it is not likely that the 'Natural Approach' would be suitable for children in the Silent Period.

'Total Physical Response'

This is a method of teaching a second language developed by James Asher (Asher 2009). It follows Krashen's principles of comprehensible input; learners are given physical commands to carry out, and when the learner correctly carries out the instruction, they are given positive feedback and more detailed instructions. No language output at all is required on the part of the student; it is assumed that with adequate input, the student will learn the language. There is no explicit teaching of vocabulary or grammar.

The method could be suitable for young children, as it provides an enjoyable physical activity in which the silent child would be able to participate simply by following what the other children are doing; the students are not required to speak in response to the instructions. The silent child might therefore, in this method, find it possible to carry out the physical movements, and in this way not only pick up on the language being used but also be part of a group of children who are all doing the same thing – perhaps a very limited form of social interaction but at least it is some level of social participation through joining in with others' activities.

The limitation of this method is that the vocabulary and the type of grammatical structures used (the imperative) are limited to the physical actions, and do not provide a sufficient sample of the social use of language for the child to learn the to-and-fro of interactive conversation, or any vocabulary other than that relating to movement.

Teaching Proficiency through Reading and Storytelling (TPRS)

This is a method originally based on the comprehensible input theories of Krashen (1981) but with considerable additional development which make it a 'usage-based' theory rather than a purely 'input' theory.

I will cover this method in greater detail than the previously-mentioned programmes, as in one specific way it has similarities to the StoryFrames programme: the programme makes use of narrative (stories) as a significant part of the teaching methodology.

TPRS was originally based on the Total Physical Response method (see above) but was significantly modified. The developer of the programme, Blaine Ray (Ray 2004) felt that TPR was too limited in terms of the range of language provided when the teacher gave instructions only for physical movements.

The TPRS method uses simple stories, appropriate to the child's level and interests, to help students to use, in spoken form, the words and grammatical structures which have been provided as input through the story.

The method includes extensive repetition of language structures, elicited by asking the children questions about the story they have just heard. Every question is phrased with slight modifications in order to expand the structures being heard and used, and the effect of this repetition is crucial to the efficacy of the learning.

The first step in this method is for the teacher to present the material (usually, but not always, a story) using visual props (such as illustrations or puppets) and gesture, to make sure the student understands what is being talked about.

Through carefully targeted and varied types of questioning, the teacher then elicits a repetition of the story from the student. As the details get filled in, the repetition of the basic sentence structure continues, with the sentences being slowly and carefully expanded, one step at a time, to provide additional input and output of the vocabulary and grammar, while remaining in the context of the now-familiar story. The idea is that is it more effective to learn a small number of language targets really well, instead of a large number of targets which are soon forgotten ("narrow and deep instead of broad and shallow": Lichtman 2018).

The story provides interest for the student, and the co-construction of a story provides some social interaction and personal involvement which therefore further motivates the student. This kind of co-construction of story (in TPRS theory this is called "asking a story", as multiple and repeated questions are at the heart of the story session) is very different from the kind of prescriptive role-play exercises of many standard second-language teaching methods.

The goal of this method is "to scaffold language so that it remains completely comprehensible and accessible to students, resulting in successful and relatively rapid acquisition of the language. A constant flow of scaffolded input ensures that students will understand every message and be able to respond successfully, whether it is with a simple 'yes' or 'no', one word, or an entire phrase or sentence. Input may take the form of graduated questions, circling questions, personalised questions, cooperatively created stories, mini-stories, short stories, fairy tales, sequences, songs, poems, rhymes, chants and a wide variety of readings" (Gaab 2021).

The TPRS method is one which is very effective indeed in teaching a second language to a confident and outgoing student. It is also easily adaptable to small groups or to the single child. However, in terms of working with the silent child, the TPRS method is likely to be rather too direct, in that it requires at least some output on the part of the student, from very early on in the programme.

For this reason, TPRS is not likely to be suitable for the silent child who will be unlikely to manage any output at all, and who may in fact be intimidated by such demands. For a child in the Silent Period, the repetitive questioning may be more likely to be perceived as threatening than as a motivating teaching strategy.

In summary, as we have said above, any teaching programme based on linguistic aims alone is not likely to be effective in supporting the silent child, due to the complex mix of socio-cultural and personality issues involved in the Silent Period. A more multi-disciplinary programme is indicated. It is for this reason that the StoryFrames programme was developed.

***

CHAPTER 4

The StoryFrames programme

The aims of the programme

The aims of the StoryFrames programme are:

- to assist the silent child to integrate socially as well as academically at school
- to support the child in emerging from the Silent Period

The programme approaches the issue of the Silent Period using a multi-disciplinary and integrated approach to language and communication, as described in Chapter Two. This type of theory does not view the development of emotion, cognition, language, social skills and play as separate or modular, but as inextricably interconnected.

For this reason, the StoryFrames programme cannot be defined as a programme whose main aim is to teach a second language.

The programme was devised to support the simultaneous development of linguistic and social interaction skills, in the strong belief that these are inseparable, and act in feedback loops with each other. These feedback loops work in various ways, and act on each other simultaneously.

One feedback loop works in this way: if we take as a starting point that the silent child can be helped to develop a sense of the confidence or agency needed to approach other children in play, then this interaction with other children provides the silent child with opportunities for language output. This in turn leads to further language facility for this child, which leads to increased social interaction.

Another feedback loop takes as a starting point the response of the other children to the silent child: if the other children view the silent child as someone not likely to interact or play, they will be less likely to approach and include this child. If intervention can encourage the silent child to be more willing to interact, the perception of this child by other children will start to change. As a result, more opportunities will be made available by other children, which can result in the silent child's increased social participation, which in turn provides the child with more opportunities for language output, and thus increased language learning, which leads to ever greater social interaction.

The structure of the StoryFrames programme

In choosing how to approach the intervention with these silent children, it was necessary to choose a language structure which would be socially interactive, and at the same time would have a specific, definable structure which could be mediated in a short time to a young child.

For this reason, it was decided to use narrative as the basic 'tool' for the programme, as it meets both of these requirements.

The use of the narrative form

The tendency of humans to use story, myth and legend has been documented historically and has been found in all cultures (Campbell 1988, Donald 1991); research shows that humans are natural storytellers. The social use of narrative is assumed to be an evolutionary development dating back to the beginnings of settled human cultures (Boyd 2005). The narrative form is still used in spoken if not written forms to transmit myths about a culture and its origins to the next generation in extant hunter-gatherer societies. Stories need not be written in books to be stories.

Humans are interested in stories, and use stories to communicate socially. People spend socially interactive time telling other people about their experiences or plans or wishes, and listening to other people telling their stories. Human beings in all cultures use narrative forms to talk about how things should be done and about what is important in that culture.

Different cultures have their own favourite children's stories (Bruner 1986). Stories are used by human beings to "guide and shape the way we experience our daily lives, to communicate with other people, and to develop relationships with them" (Engel 1995 p. 25). Being able to tell one's story means being able to give voice to oneself, and to be heard by others. It is a vital part of our social and emotional health.

By narrative, or "stories", we mean not just fictional stories in books, but our own stories; the stories we tell about who we are, what we love and fear, what we are interested in, and what we hope for. Stories can be autobiographical ("Let me tell you why I chose to go there for my holiday") or fictional ("Once upon a time there was...") or historical ("This is what happened here, 82 years ago.")

Fivush (2022) puts it this way: narrative enables us to consider, and to tell, "...who we are in the world and who we want to be." For Bruner, "...narrative deals with the vicissitudes of human intentions." Through narratives, we are enabled to express what we know about ourselves, about others, and about life (Bruner 1986).

In order to tell these stories, we need language. Of course gesture and pictures play their part, but the human evolution that has led to modern society and community has at the same time advanced our use of language and led to our using language to tell our stories (Boyd 2009).

Merlin Donald (1991) believes that language evolved in humans in response to the social need for narrative, in order to enable the transmission of a collective version of reality within a tribe or society. He goes so far as to describe narrative skill as "...the driving force behind language use" (Donald 1991 p. 257).

From their earliest years as speakers of a language, children begin to narrate stories. These begin as stories about what we did today, or what we might do next. This has been shown to be an important aspect of their socio-cultural development (Bruner 1986, Nelson 1996, Nelson and Fivush 2020, Fivush 2022). The modes and uses of narrative are learned by children through experiencing everyday social interactions and conversations with their family. Wells (1985) and Bruner (1986) have shown how listening to and telling stories help children to realise the symbolic power of language to create both real and fantasy worlds.

Taking this view of narrative, we see that narrative is not solely a matter for the person creating the story. Creating and telling a story is an interactive activity; it involves a listener too. We use narrative to share our memories, feelings, hopes or ideas with another person.

In terms of the social use of language, telling a story therefore requires the narrator to take into account the needs of the listener, and to behave in ways which will involve the listener in the story. This requires the narrator to attend to the listener, as much as the listener attends to the narrator. The narrator needs to show the "attention and intention" as defined by Tomasello (2003) in order to make sure that the listener is interested, and can understand what is being said. This is where language comes in: the child needs to learn how to use linguistic 'tools' to introduce, describe, sequence, explain and end a story.

Only once we have language can we tell our story. Here we find another feedback loop. Bruner shows how language and narrative mutually affect each other: the acquisition of language enables narrative, and narrative enables the further development of language (Bruner 1986). Hearing and telling narratives also develop cognitive skills such as sequencing, cause and effect links, and inference. This leads to our being able to tell ever more complex stories, using ever more complex language.

There is something about the narrative form which brings together the thoughts, feelings and wishes of the narrator, and draws these to the attention of the listener. Narratives organise ideas and feelings into a theme; the plot, the events and the way the characters behave all unite to bring this theme home to the narrator as well as to the listener. Marsten et al (2016) put it this way: "Narratives home in."

Boyce (2019) in talking about how children use and present narratives in their play, says "we tell about things that scare us, because it makes them gradually less scary; about sadness, because it makes the sadness diminish a little each time we do. Our long-gone forebears surely sat, themselves, on dark winter nights around hearths and fires and told each other of narrow escapes, frightful adversaries, and how they almost didn't make it. And even then, there must have been not just comfort but protection in the telling."

There is also a private aspect in narrative, in which we in effect tell ourselves stories about what matters to us; we think through or ruminate on things that have happened, or things that are important to us. Nelson and Fivush (2020) refer to the "dual function" of narrative: on one hand outward facing, in which the child tells or shares their narrative to others, and on the other hand inward facing, in which the language of narrative provides the child with a tool to organise their own internal feelings and thoughts.

This is seen as a crucial aspect in the child's development of a sense of identity, and through this, of the child's willingness to interact with others. This "private narrative" will be seen in the early stages of the StoryFrames programme, in which the child, playing with a set of toys, enacts without speaking a story about this pretend play.

In the StoryFrames programme we make use of a small set of carefully chosen toys (see the section on play below) and a small set of age-appropriate illustrated children's books (see Chapter 5 below for more information about the choice of books.)

Because the narrative form was chosen as the basic structure for the StoryFrames programme, it is the development of the child's narrative which is one of the ways in which the success of the programme can be measured. At the point where the programme is seen to be most successful, the narratives which emerge in the sessions become jointly created by both the teacher and the child. The co-creation of narrative, which takes the form of a shared conversation between equals, with all the qualities of a satisfactory communicative experience for both participants, is evidence of the significant progress the child has made in both social and linguistic terms.

Narrative structure can scaffold language acquisition

While many published programmes teaching a second language use an open-ended range of teaching materials such as free conversation, songs, and questions, the StoryFrames programme uses mainly narrative. This could be seen as a limitation, but there are specific reasons for this choice.

The idea is that having a clear structure can provide "organising principles" (Jang et al 2010) which make the scope for the language being learned less vast, less open-ended, and more accessible. Jang et al (2010) suggest that such a constraint, provided by a single, clear structure, makes it more likely that the child will be able to make use of the experience: the aims of each session are clear, and the child quickly learns what is involved. The child can focus on one specific structure instead of dealing with the vast number of possibilities which are available in spontaneous language. Too much structure is constricting and can be intrusive, while too little is not supportive. The StoryFrames programme attempts to strike a balance between the two.

There is considerable evidence of the facilitative role of narrative in learning a second language (for example, Amer, 1992; Hall et al, 2005). The scaffold, or structure, sets out for the child a narrative flow, a sequence of ideas travelling in time. This facilitates the expansion of their ideas or thoughts; these ideas, moving along an imaginary timeline, provide a sequenced structure into which words and sentences can be 'slotted'. In this respect story acts as a "vehicle" (Garvie 1990): narrative is used as a carrier or platform, providing opportunities for verbal interaction and language (see also Nelson 1996, Whitehurst et al 1988).

The programme uses a small set of miniature toys (here called 'tiny toys') which the child is free to play with. Most silent children will spontaneously begin to play with these toys, and most of them create, through their pretend play, a narrative sequence of events. This is the 'private narrative' referred to earlier (Nelson and Fivush 2020.)

In learning a second language, the tasks of simultaneously deciding *what* to say, and also *how* to say it, combine to make spoken language difficult: the speaker has to deal with two very different cognitive tasks at the same time. When we have a narrative structure, which the child has just created in their pretend play, the aspect of *what* to say is provided ready-made: it is the private story that the child has just enacted in their pretend play.

Stories usually make use of a specific set of linguistic structures to relate a sequence of events in time. The analysis of these structures comes under the heading of "Story Grammar" (Stein and Glenn 1979, Rumelhart 1980) which lists the various elements usually found in a story. These might include, among others, introducing the characters who participate in the story, and a description of the place and time in which the story takes place. There is also usually a plot, which describes how the characters interact with each other, and there is often a problem to be solved, and a description of the feelings of the characters when they approach the problem and after they have solved the problem. There is usually a clear beginning, indicated by various narrative starting formulae, and an ending, similarly indicated by various ending formulae.

For younger children, and especially children of pre-school age, these story elements are often only beginning to emerge in the stories they tell. Stories at this age might be more like collections of events, or of observations, without any clear plot linking them together (Applebee 1978).

The stories told by the two children who took part in the original research project exemplify this. Child A, who was almost five years old, included in her stories aspects of traditional Story Grammar: there is a problem to be overcome, and a description of how the characters in the stories approach the problem, and how they feel during repeated attempts to solve the problem. The presence of these aspects of Story Grammar was apparent from the outset in the pretend play of this child, even before she had the language to present the narrative verbally.

The younger child, Child B, started the programme at age 3, and his stories were brief, repetitive and often disconnected from each other. If there was a hint of a plot, it was often meandering, but more often there was just a series of seemingly disconnected events. Child B's stories in the early sessions moved from topic to topic, seemingly in jumbled order, without any clear causal or temporal links.

This kind of narrative is called "leapfrog narrative" (McCabe 1997) or "heaps" (Applebee 1978). This is to be expected around age 3, and at no time did the programme attempt to help him develop his stories beyond the level which was age-appropriate for him. It is important to stress that the intention of using narrative in the programme is *not* to help the child to develop more mature story grammar; there is no wish to move a child beyond what is age-appropriate. The use of narrative in the StoryFrames programme is in order to provide for the child a "scaffold" (Bruner 1986): a structure or platform, on which the child can build, and begin to use language.

In terms of benefits for cognitive development, and for the development of abstract concepts, there is also a value in that narratives are situated in time. Time is a very abstract concept and one which is difficult to put into words; the way time is expressed in language is usually through using metaphors of space and of the body moving through space. Different languages use very different metaphors (Hofstadter and Sander 2013). The experience of having narratives told about their pretend play therefore also contributes towards the child's ability to use more abstract language.

Using the narrative form to develop a sense of self and of agency

There is also an emotional aspect in the movement of narrative through time. Our sense of identity is based largely on our autobiographical experience. During the StoryFrames sessions, when we are observing the silent child, we may see them acting out aspects of something they might have experienced in the past, or something which they are feeling currently. Pretend play provides an opportunity for the child to process these memories and these ideas, and to experience the associated feelings. The repeated play with the same toys, and the repetition of similar stories, which seems to be so prevalent in the play of young children, offers the option to re-visit and perhaps change the sequence or the outcome of a narrative by introducing other ideas, choices and outcomes. This is a concept on which the psychological therapy method called "Narrative Therapy" is based (Morgan 2000).

This alternative telling of one's story (Marsten et al 2016) can help the child to develop a sense of identity which might include a greater feeling of agency: the feeling that they can choose and perhaps even control what happens around them, and to them. For the silent child who has had to make a transition between one country and another, and between one language and another, narrative can provide support in bridging these events and helping to integrate them into their current identity. We will see hints of this in the transcripts, provided below, of actual stories told by the two children in the original StoryFrames research programme.

The concept of agency in learning is at the core of this programme. Agency in learning "involves being empowered and able to contribute to the direction and form that learning takes…. agency arises from the interaction between enabling environments, supportive relationships and an inner experience" (Le Courtois and Baker 2023). As will be shown below, in the description of how to carry out the StoryFrames programme, this empowerment of the child to make choices in the sessions (whether to play or not to play, whether to speak or not to speak, whether to listen to a story or not to) works towards building the sense of agency and of learner empowerment which is crucial in helping the child emerge from the Silent Period.

Little (1991) refers to "learner autonomy" and the consideration of allowing a learner to choose their own timing and way of entering a new language community. Instead of viewing the child as a passive receiver of information, such an approach sees the child as a naturally curious learner, who benefits from being engaged in activities which are to some extent of their own choosing, under the guidance of a teacher who observes the child's development, and by following the child's lead supports the child in the direction that the child is moving. The child is seen as a participant in learning, rather than as a recipient.

Engel suggests that narrative helps in developing a sense of agency in the narrator, because narrative can make possible "…the imaginative control you gain over the world by being able to decide, at least symbolically, who does what to whom and what things look like and sound like." (Engel 1995)

Engel further suggests that stories not only reconstruct and communicate experience but actually "*are* experience" in themselves. Through the stories we tell, especially those we tell about ourselves, we construct and re-construct the way we behave and feel.

Similarly, Cattanach writes that "telling stories and playing stories can be a way of controlling our world and what happens to us in that world and for a child who lacks power it can be an enriching experience. For once the child can say 'I'm the king of the castle, and you're the dirty rascal,' and not live the consequences in their reality world." (Cattanach 2008).

Similarly, Nelson and Fivush (2020) see narrative, and specifically autobiographical narrative, as being able to provide a "bridge across time" for the narrator and for the listener: creating "a sense of expanded self through time".

It is this sense of agency which is something that the silent and socially isolated child might need to develop in order to be able to express their ideas, feelings and needs.

Of course, one could suggest that the silence of these children is, in fact, the expression of their sense of agency: they have made a decision about how they will live in this new and unfamiliar world, and by not talking, they have decided in some way to separate themselves from it. This is what Winnicott (2018) claims when he talks of the right *not* to communicate, and what Granger (2004) says about silent children having a right to choose their own response to the events in their lives.

However, if we think about agency as the feeling that we can choose and perhaps even control what happens around us and to us, then it is hard to make a case for the Silent Period being an expression of agency. If it is the case that the child is *able* to communicate and interact freely, but is making a choice to be silent, perhaps that would indeed be an expression of agency. In the case of these silent children, however, who have neither the language needed for communication, nor the confidence to try to communicate, even non-verbally, it is hard to see how enabling them to communicate socially can be anything but a way to support their individual agency.

What we would wish for these silent children is that they develop a sufficiently strong sense of agency which would, in the words of Tomasello (2022) enable them to "be capable of choosing to act or not to act."

***

The use of pretend play in the StoryFrames programme

In the StoryFrames programme the child is, in every session, offered the same set of carefully chosen "tiny toys" (see the section on Equipment, below) to use as they wish to. With one exception (a small set of building blocks or bricks), these are not construction toys, nor are they 'physical activity' toys such as bats or balls. They are miniature toys, representing people, animals and objects from the real world.

Play, and especially pretend play, is a very important agent in the social, emotional and cognitive development of the child. (Broadhead 2004; Fabian and Mou 2009; Forbes 2004). In pretend play, children start to use symbolisation (using an object and pretending it is something else) and analogy (attributing to an object the properties of something else). They are starting to work in Piaget's Pre-operational stage (Piaget 1954) where they begin to use imagination and abstract thinking: they can now refer to invisible, imagined or possible objects or events, and to move on from the focus of the younger child on the 'here-and-now' towards the 'there-and-then.' They are also developing hypothetical thinking: What if..? What might happen? What could happen?

Vygotsky, in his analysis of what play means to the young child, says that in infancy, prior to the development of the ability to play, the child expects and demands immediate gratification of their needs. Once the child reaches the age of around three, they begin to realise that their immediate needs might not be met. However they do not give up on the desire for immediate gratification of their needs. This, according to Vygotsky, is where play comes in: it provides the child with a way to express the "imaginary, illusory realization of unrealizable desires" (Vygotsky 2023). Through the development of a capacity for imagination, the child finds a way to think about the gratification of desires, and can make up a kind of story about how it would be, if that were possible.

Pretend play also utilises and develops the child's theory of mind: when they are playing a character, or participating in role play, they are putting themselves in another's shoes and considering how other people's minds may be different from their own. Cattanach writes, "The use of narratives and stories in play can help children to make sense of their own lives and also to learn empathy through imagining how other characters in their stories might feel" (Cattanach 2008).

Further benefits of pretend play result from the narratives which emerge almost spontaneously during the play, and which include the cognitive skills of sequencing and cause-effect logic: what happens first, next and last, and the consequences of events which explain why things happen. This is the time in which the child develops logical reasoning, problem-solving and hypothetical thinking.

The tiny toys used in the StoryFrames programme are carefully selected to serve as hints, or 'nudges' for the child to create their own story, expressing their own concerns, thoughts and feelings. Baker et al (2021) suggest that "…playful learning makes space for children's agency in their learning by giving children control and engaging them as willing participants."

Danon-Boileau (2001) provides extensive discussion of his use of toys in therapy. He recommends always making play equipment available to the child, and always following the child's lead, letting the child make choices about what to do during the sessions. The teacher should be a passive observer of the child's play, taking an interest but not intervening.

Because the narratives emerge from the child's own pretend play, there is an intrinsic motivation at work: they are talking about their own interests. This kind of playful learning has been shown to enable children to feel a sense of control and of agency, and to feel that they are active participants in their learning, instead of passive recipients (Perry 2013). For the child who has recently been moved out of their familiar home, culture and language, and who has been a passive participant in the decisions or the tragedies of their families, this development of a sense of agency is crucial to their emerging from the silence.

Boyce (2019) writes that "…play, like dreaming, is a way of bringing realities down to size, a means of emptying the poison from fraught conflicts and indignities." He explains that it is through play that children learn who they are and form their identities; they use play to work through the hurts and difficulties in their lives.

Play and the development of language

Research has shown that pretend play, language and literacy are connected by common cognitive processes (Pellegrini 1985). As the play becomes more complex, it becomes more and more embedded in language, and makes greater use of emerging narrative skills (Roskos 1990). Kuczaj (1982) makes the point that "play affords opportunities to practice language", so that while the primary benefits of play are cognitive and emotional, an additional benefit is the development of language. Pretend play can be a very effective and enabling way to develop the language of narrative, and should be intentionally used by educators as a language teaching resource (Roskos 1990 p 510).

It was found, in the initial research using the StoryFrames programme, that once the children learned to represent their play in language, they also began gaining confidence to speak out and actively tell their stories, instead of being passive listeners to someone else's stories. A sense of personal agency was clearly emerging.

Shared play

Pretend play, or imaginative play, can be something a child does on their own, without communicating or sharing with anyone else; this is typical of normally developing younger children who, in their early days at nursery, may play alongside other children but take time to communicate and share with others. However, as children develop, their pretend play becomes a shared social activity. In the StoryFrames programme, both solitary play and shared play are seen: initially the silent child plays on their own, and as the programme develops, they gradually begin to share their play with the teacher. The transition from solitary play to shared play is a crucial part of the programme. It mirrors that of normal development, where children start to play with others instead of merely alongside others.

Heath (1985) describes this kind of shared pretend play as a socio-dramatic experience.

Narratives emerge spontaneously during imaginative play involving more than one child. The play then involves talking about imaginary events using a variety of types of talk (cohesion devices, narrative introductions, sounds and noises). This kind of shared and verbal imaginative play occurs naturally among children who are acquiring a first language, and it is a crucial part of their social development. It is clear therefore that any programme for silent and isolated children must ensure that they too are given opportunities to participate in this kind of shared socio-dramatic play. Boyce (2019) credits children's shared imaginative play with enabling them to creatively explore their own lives and the lives of others, to learn social skills such as navigating peer groups and learning to compromise with their friend's needs.

How pretend play and narrative work together

We see therefore that the use of narrative and the use of tiny toys in pretend play are actually one single method, and inseparable from each other. The impetus for the narratives is pretend play: the stories emerge naturally and spontaneously out of the child's pretend play activity.

Importantly, Paley (1981, 1990) erases the distinctions between play and storytelling, claiming that for the young child, the two are inextricably linked. "It is play, of course, but it is also story in action, just as storytelling is play put into narrative form" (Paley 1990 p 4). Pretend play is therefore, according to Paley, actually the child's "real and serious world, the stage upon which any identity is possible and secret thoughts can be safely revealed" (1990 p 7).

Cattanach (2008) echoes Paley's ideas, describing pretend play as "the reality of the child's actual life", through which the child can express wishes, fears and hopes. She claims that children play and tell stories not only to represent experience as they know it, but also "to represent experience as they would like it to be".

Pretend play is therefore a crucially important part of the learning and development of young children, as it promotes both cognitive and emotional development.

In the original StoryFrames project, the potential of the combined benefits of pretend play and narrative to enable the silent child to reconstruct a new, more assertive identity emerged in the children's stories, with themes of mastery and power, or the lack of it, appearing repeatedly. In their pretend play they enacted situations of deep emotion: sometimes violent, and sometimes full of longing. It was clear, from observing the repetition of these themes week after week, that they were enacting what was of concern to them, perhaps events which they remembered, or perhaps a reality they wished for.

Here is a transcript of one of the early sessions with Child A. At this stage of the programme, she was enjoying playing with the toys provided, and was just beginning to say some words and phrases aloud.

Speaker	Transcript
	[The child chooses to play with some animals and the miniature furniture. She picks up her own big soft toy, a turtle, which she has brought with her to school]
CHILD A	A big, big bed!
TEACHER	This one? [The teacher offers her a cushion which is the right size for the turtle]
CHILD A	Yeah
TEACHER	What else?
CHILD A	[The child points to a sign affixed to the wall] What says no?
TEACHER	[There is a sign affixed to the wall, and the teacher assumes she is asking what the sign means. It is similar to a 'no parking' sign, with a red diagonal stripe across a circle, and a picture of a sandwich crossed out] It means no eating food in this room.
CHILD A	[Goes back to the toys] Blanket?
TEACHER	[The teacher offers her the two soft cloths from the toy set, which can be used as a blanket] Big blanket or small blanket?
CHILD A	Big one – so big! [she opens her arms wide]

We see here the beginning of a narrative: the turtle who wants to sleep and needs a blanket; perhaps something about needing a place of warmth and comfort. She also expresses concern about the sign on the wall, which may be something important that she needs to know but does not understand, and this is perhaps making her anxious.

We also see the beginnings of a plot in this pretend play. The child spontaneously developed the same story further in a later session.

Speaker	Transcript
	[The child chooses a few animals to play with but there is only one miniature bed. She has again brought her own turtle toy to school and has it with her.]
CHILD A	Oh, they can't sleep, they need to sleep on another one [points to the bed] like that! And then came turtle and what did he say? I wanna sleep too!
TEACHER	I wanna sleep too. So he got in the bed.
CHILD A	And then was coming a frog. [sic]
TEACHER	And then a frog came, and he said...
CHILD A	I wanna sleep too! Then another froggy came.
	[The child continues to take from the toy box more and more animals who try to sleep in the bed; they don't all fit on the bed no matter how hard she tries to get them on the bed simultaneously]
CHILD A	Look! Look the froggies are not sleeping and the geckoes and the turtles! They can't sleep.
TEACHER	What can they do?
CHILD A	They need to try!! [She is now using a louder voice, for the first time, having previously used only a very quiet voice. She makes a gesture of despair with her hands, and a very expressive facial expression showing upset.]

These two consecutive stories show how this child's pretend play, and the stories she told during this play, expressed what was of interest and concern to her at the time. The narrative form, as used by children, enables the creation of an autobiographical consciousness: "The story I tell myself" or the story about the self (Barnes 1997).

The stories that a young child tells present a kind of "self-portrait" of that child (Engel 1995) and through this the teacher is better able to understand the child. Note however that the teacher makes no attempt to insert interpretations of what the child is thinking or feeling into the interaction. This is of paramount importance. This is not psychotherapy or play therapy. While our tentative interpretations may add to our understanding of each particular child, they play no part in the method and must be kept to ourselves. Our job is merely to facilitate and to witness the child's own pretend play and the child's own story.

The role of parents and teachers in developing the child's narrative skills

There is much evidence from research which shows that teachers and parents play a critical role in shaping their children's ability to develop narrative skills. For example, Peterson and McCabe (1983) found that parents who talk about past and recent experiences to their children, or tell elaborate stories, have children who do this too.

We are exposed to narrative from our earliest years. Parents coming home from an afternoon at the park will talk to their children about what they did, what they saw, and how it felt. They are recalling a past event. When planning to go out, parents may talk in the future tense about what they will see, where they will be going, and what they will do there. This too is a form of narrative, with a clear sequence of events, and clear intentions on the part of the participants. From a very early age, therefore, children learn that their personal experience can be recorded or retold in language, through the medium of narrative (Nelson 1996).

Cattanach (2008) suggests that the very act of creating a story that is listened to and accepted by a sympathetic listening person is therapeutic. She comments on the special quality of the relationship between a storyteller and a listener, with the story acting "as a way to negotiate a shared meaning between the two". This suggests that much can be done through teacher-child interaction to promote the development of narrative skills, as well as the development of social interaction.

In the StoryFrames sessions, the teacher makes no suggestions as to how the child should use the toys, and does not attempt to interpret the story to the child. This sensitive acceptance by the teacher of whatever story or pretend play the child wishes to enact serves to validate the child's feelings and to strengthen the child's sense of agency. The teacher, in the early stages of the programme, listens attentively to the child, and does not attempt to provide a model of spoken language.

In this way, the StoryFrames programme differs from a traditional speech and language therapy session, in which there would usually be clear speech or language targets to be worked on.

Another way to describe how this programme works is in the words of Engel (1995). She talks of the need for educators to "create a space" where the child is encouraged to tell stories, in order for the child "to feel a robust sense of power and ownership, to feel that [they] can tell all kinds of stories to express all kinds of meanings". It is this kind of space, and the use of story to help develop the sense of "power and ownership" which is a major part of the design of the StoryFrames programme. The StoryFrames method creates an interactive and supportive relationship between teacher and child, and it is this relationship which becomes a catalyst for their overcoming the silence.

The widespread acceptance of the use of narrative in education finds voice in the words of the narrative theorist Nicolopoulou, who strongly promotes the use of fantasy play and narrative in education: she talks of the use of stories "written *for* children, told *to* children, constructed by teachers *with* children, and composed and told *by* children." (Nicolopoulou, 1997 p. 179).

***

CHAPTER 5

Setting up the StoryFrames programme

The programme works through providing the child with carefully graded exposure to interaction with one other person. This principle of graded exposure is in a way similar to that used in some psychological therapies.

Initially, the child will avoid any feared situation, as we all tend to avoid anything which might be threatening. Through gradually increasing the exposure of the child to the talk of one specific teacher, the child becomes habituated to the teacher talking in their presence. In other words, the programme starts with how much the teacher talks, and not with how much the child talks.

The teacher is, at this stage, not giving the child instructions and not trying to elicit an answer. The teacher simply presents the set of tiny toys and the picture books, and invites the child to play, if they want to, or to listen while the teacher reads to them from a picture book, if that is what they prefer.

The child starts the programme by doing something which is not threatening: playing with toys, not being asked to talk, and not being in the presence of people who might talk and expect an answer. In this way we hope to provide for the child a feeling of safety and security, in which there is no threat at all. Threat, for the child in the Silent Period, is assumed to be any situation in which the child might be expected to talk, but cannot.

We enter the child's silence and witness their silent play. We begin to make our presence felt in the space. The next step, tentatively taken during the course of the programme, is where the teacher gradually begins to add words, and later sentences, and then a model of a story structure, but always in relation to what the child is doing in their pretend play, and never demanding that the child speak. We are working towards helping children to feel comfortable in the presence of talk, even while they themselves might remain silent.

Once the child begins to play with the toys, the adult manages their own talk in very specific stages. These carefully graded steps are described in full in Chapters 7-12, below.

When the teacher does talk, it is not the idle talk that a child might overhear when sitting near other people; this is talk which relates directly to the child's own pretend play. The teacher's talk in the programme is very subtly managed so as not to be intrusive, but at the same time, to relate to the child. We want to show the child that we are interested in what they are doing, but will not expect the child to talk if they do not wish to. This gradual exposure to interaction through talk enables the child to begin to habituate to the situation of being in the presence of a person who speaks a different language.

According to the theory of graded exposure and habituation, the child's level of anxiety is reduced, simply by continuing to be present in the feared situation over time. The child can then learn a new way of being with other people, and can develop a more realistic perception of the classroom and school situation as a place which is not threatening.

***

How we begin the programme

This section is a general introduction to the sequential steps of the programme; a more detailed description will be provided in subsequent chapters.

We start by providing a quiet and secluded space, a space which will remain consistent throughout the programme, in order to promote for the child a sense of safety and continuity. This carefully contrived space, and the graded strategies used in the programme, provide these children with an "affordance" (Gibson 1979) - a situation in the environment which precisely matches the child's needs and capability at that time, and which thereby provides the support needed for the child to feel relaxed and not fearful, and to begin to develop their communication skills in the new world in which they have arrived.

We then present the child with a very carefully chosen set of miniature toys, and the child is invited to play. The child is not directed in any way as to which toys to choose or how to play with them.

The teacher gradually begins to use words, phrases and then sentences to describe what the child is doing in their pretend play. This provides some language input, but always referring to and relating to the child's own pretend play, and never expecting or demanding that the child speaks.

The teacher is thus mediating how we can put play into language. It is this mediation between the play and its associated language which is crucial for young children who are reluctant to use language at all; the teacher uses language to simply describe what it is that they are imagining in their play. This is not necessarily a communicative form of language; that comes later in the programme.

Gradually, as the child becomes more confident, through having played out their stories and having heard the teacher describing their stories, the child gradually and spontaneously begins to use language to speak more and more about their own play and their own stories.

The programme is thus sequential, beginning from a position of a fully-accepted silence, and following the principle of graded exposure of the child to the once-feared situation of social interaction through language.

It is possible, and often necessary, to introduce flexibility into the programme by taking a step back if we feel the child is showing signs of anxiety. This is especially indicated if the child, even after having started to speak more freely, indicates in some way that they wish to return to a silent stage and to do some more solitary play. In such a case, returning to an earlier stage is not to be seen as a regression, but rather as the child's needing additional consolidation of their skills before moving on.

The important thing is not to push the child towards speaking before they are ready. Reducing the emotional pressure on the child to speak is a vital aspect in the success of the programme.

Duration of the programme

For this programme to be successful, it is recommended that most children need at least 10 sessions of about 20-30 minutes each, preferably bi-weekly. The benefits of "little and often", that is, shorter sessions, more frequently than once a week, are in the cumulative effects of this kind of intervention (Feuerstein 2015). This provides the child with a repeated and consistent experience of enjoyable social interaction in the new language. A week's break between sessions is too long a period for a small child to be able to remember or connect with what was done in the previous session.

Depending on issues of cost and timing, each stage of the programme can be expanded over any number of sessions, and the entire programme can be drawn out over time for as long as desired. The ultimate aim is not to get through the programme, but rather to gradually and sensitively bring the child to a place of confidence where they can play freely with other children and participate in a relaxed manner in the learning experiences of the classroom.

It is of course not possible to predict how much change one can effect in this or any programme. In some cases there is rapid progress, but of course each child is an individual, and ideally one would be able to continue the programme until the child becomes at least adequately socially integrated and communicative in the classroom. The original research project was run over the duration of one school term (two sessions per week for six weeks) and that amount of time was found to be very effective for those two children.

Taking into account that speech and language therapy is expensive, and that there are often long waiting lists, it is a great help to have a programme such as this which can differentiate those children who can use the support effectively, from those who might need more specifically targeted types of speech and language therapy or psychological intervention. If, after six weeks of this programme, a child does not make the expected communicative progress, is still socially isolated, and is speaking very little or not at all to other children and teachers, please do contact a speech and language therapist.

Equipment

The StoryFrames programme uses a very specific set of play equipment. The equipment consists of a set of carefully-chosen but easily available and inexpensive miniature toys ("tiny toys"), and a small set of commonly-used children's picture books which most pre-schools will already have in their classrooms.

"Tiny Toys": The set of toys used in this programme

To use the StoryFrames method is to make a deliberate choice in favour of intervention in the play of the child, but in a very specific way: not to change their play in any way, not to join in or to direct it, but to always follow the child's lead, and to use the child's play as a basic platform from which to develop social interaction. The StoryFrames programme deliberately makes use of only miniature toys, as opposed to full-scale toys.

Of course, the child is free to play outside of the therapy sessions, during the rest of the school day, with whichever they choose; it is only during the StoryFrames sessions that the play is restricted to the set of toys provided within this programme.

Regular-sized toys, which are not at the miniature scale of dolls'-house toys, are also useful and enjoyable in general play situations, and it could be said that the miniatures are simply a practical and convenient way to include an entire world in a small box, allowing the child to explore the world from a safe place.

But the choice of miniatures here is deliberate. The miniature toys seem to encourage the child's use of imagination. With tiny toys, children seem to feel freed from everyday reality, and more able to imagine the miniature as any other creature, in any imagined situation, than they can with full-sized toys. Miniatures are as far removed from reality as possible, considering that any toy doll or toy car of any size is of course a replica of reality. The small size seems to give children the feeling that they can control their environment, and can make decisions, and re-create the world as they see it, or wish it could be.

These miniature toys are usually referred to in schools and pre-schools as 'small world' play sets. Many schools agree that the use of miniatures enables children to explore the world in a way which might not be possible with full-scale toys.

This concept is well-described by Taylor (2016) in his description of the educational programme "Mantle of the Expert" (an educational programme developed in the U.K. in the 1970's by a drama teacher, Dorothy Heathcote). Taylor uses the phrase "an invitation for imagination" to describe this kind of educational approach which uses play, drama and story. The child is enabled to let their imagination run free, to create the world of their imagination and then to share it with another person. The set of miniature toys serves this purpose for the child: it offers an invitation for them to use their imagination, to step away for a moment from the school setting, and to create whatever world they wish to create.

A question which sometimes arises is whether this is a kind of psychological play therapy. The StoryFrames programme is very different from psychological play therapy; play therapy is to children what counselling is to adults. Play therapy utilizes play, the child's natural medium of expression, to help them express their feelings; it is often easier to express feelings through a medium other than language. In the StoryFrames programme, however, while we also utilise toys, we have no intention of providing any kind of counselling. And unlike play therapy, the intention of StoryFrames is specifically and intentionally to move the child towards the ability to ultimately use spoken language to interact socially.

The recommended toys (see the list below) are easily available at regular toyshops, 'pound shops' or from dolls' house suppliers. They can be made of plastic, metal or wood, depending on preference, cost and availability. The main thing is that they are non-toxic, durable and safe, and have no small or sharp pieces which can injure the child or become detached and become a choking risk.

The set of toys to be used is deliberately limited in number, so that the child does not feel overwhelmed by choice. The limited choice is a constraint which acts as an "organising principle" (Jang, Reeve and Deci 2010) making it more likely that the child will be able to make use of the experience: the choices are not endless, and the child quickly becomes familiar with the toy set and knows what is involved. The child can in this way develop a sense that the sessions are consistent and predictable, and this predictability adds to the non-threatening atmosphere of the programme.

Still following the "organising principle," the toys should be carefully and neatly arranged in a lightweight box with a secure lid and with space dividers. A plastic toolbox might be suitable. Make sure the toys fit well and that each one has its own space. The arrangement should make each toy fully visible, so that the child can make deliberate choices from the full array of toys.

Some children in the programme enjoy helping the teacher to replace the toys in their exact place after each session. This is not essential, and we are not asking the child to tidy up, but for some children it seems to be part of a predictable and consistent routine which makes them feel safe, and perhaps provides for them a sense of agency, in which at least here, in these sessions, everything is under the child's control.

In the case of a situation where a child wants something else (for example, if a child wants more cars) small blank post-it notes and a pencil should be included in the equipment, so that the teacher can make a quick sketch. Often a child wants something to represent the landscape or space in which the story is taking place: a mountain or a river, for example. This is something which a quick sketch can provide.

Tiny Toys for StoryFrames
2 cars
1 emergency car (police car, fire engine or ambulance)
6 characters (3 human, 3 animal) of different sizes (small, medium, large)
2 'scary' things (e.g. snakes, spiders, dinosaurs, robots, monsters etc)
Miniature furniture: a bed, table, two chairs
Miniature food (at least 2 items); 2 plates, a spoon or fork
A small box, with or without a lid. This should be big enough to contain at least two miniature toys. Alternatively, you could provide something which the child can use to build a fence or enclosure big enough for the characters to fit into (for example long wooden blocks, or a fence from a miniature farm scene.)
2 pieces of soft cloth, big enough for the characters to hide under or to use as blankets; approximate size 10 cm x 7 cm.
1 open-bed truck or wagon, big enough to fit the cars and/or characters onto. Some children find this particularly interesting to use in very creative ways: characters might get onto the truck and escape, or go on an excursion to a new place.
A surprise character or object (not kept in the toy box; keep it hidden, in your pocket): a doll or animal which is unlike the other toys. For example, an unusual car, a butterfly, a feather, a smooth stone, a long piece of string, something golden and shiny... anything that takes your imagination. See below for how and when this is used.
Small blank post-it notes and a pencil, so that you can draw a quick sketch in case the child asks for an item or some background scenery which is not available in the toy box.

The use of illustrated children's books

In addition to the set of miniature toys, we use a small collection of age-appropriate picture books.

The picture books serve to introduce the concept of "story" as something tangible and which has some permanence: an actual book, that can be picked up and held, and which is as tangible as any toy.

In addition to books with stories, the set of picture books should also include some non-fiction books which do not have a plot, or specific named characters (i.e. do not have a Story Grammar) but rather present a cognitive theme: a collection of different animals, or of different textures, or different sizes of objects. This may seem to contradict the stated basic tool of this programme, which is to use the narrative form; however, even though our aim is to facilitate the narration of stories with the silent child, the use of story-free books is highly recommended. Many children enjoy these books; of the two children in the original research, Child B definitely preferred non-fiction books to fiction. Non-fiction children's books are often imaginatively presented, and provide extensive language input for the child.

The presence of an actual, tangible book, whether fiction or non-fiction, is in itself a way to show the possibility of the use of language at one remove from conversational language: the possibility of representing spoken language in another format: that of writing. This move towards meta-cognition is an important developmental step.

If possible, it is helpful to include picture books showing some aspect of the child's life in their previous country. This can help the child feel that there is still some aspect of their previous life which can be remembered and treasured.

The use of picture books with repetitive rhymes is a very effective way of developing language. Such books are used extensively in classrooms and in speech and language therapy, and are very helpful in teaching beginning readers. The rhyming structure supports the child's memory of the words and phrases in the text, and the repetitive nature of these books provides predictability as well as extensive repetition of comprehensible input.

The picture books can be used at any time during the programme. If the child does not want to play with the toys, or has lost interest, or if the child seems to want to end the session early, the books are a perfect way to inject a new energy into the session.

The picture books become even more relevant once we get to the later stages in the programme (see below) where we are modelling the story-telling to the child. At this stage, the books serve as a concrete model for yet another supportive aspect of this programme: we start creating hand-made books using the child's own story. The published picture books can be shown to the child, when making their own book, in order to offer them a choice of what kind of cover they would like to make, what to write on the cover, what colours to use.

Another benefit of using picture books is that they provide a move from the inner, closed world of the child's imagination (the child's own pretend play and their own story) into another realm: that of someone else's story. This is important conceptually and emotionally:

the child can perhaps start to move out of their own isolated world and see a model of other, different worlds: worlds outside of their own anxiety or shyness. They can consider the responses and thoughts of the characters in the books and perhaps come to some new thoughts of their own.

Some of the picture books used in the programme do not have to have any written text at all. In fact, there is an opinion in the research (Arizpe et al 2014) that the absence of the written text provides scope for a more imaginative and more personal interpretation of the narrative in the book. Shaun Tan, creator of many wonderful wordless picturebooks, says this about wordless picture books in his blog:

"... There is no guidance as to how the images might be interpreted, which can be quite a liberating thing. Words have a remarkable gravitational pull on our attention, and how we interpret attendant images, like captions under a press photo. Without words, an image can invite much more attention from a reader who might otherwise reach for the nearest sentence, and let that rule their imagination." (Tan 2009)

Wordless picture books can have an effect on the child which is perhaps the same effect that the tiny toys have on the child: they provide "... an act of limited suggestion, heavily dependent on a reader willing to creatively find their own meaning." Tan further writes that "I realise that I share with many other illustrators a fundamental interest in ideas of silence and voicelessness." (Tan 2009)

In using wordless picturebooks within the StoryFrames programme, the teacher is free to tell the story to the child according to their own personal interpretation of the images, and the child, if later re-telling the story, can in turn make their own personal interpretations of the narrative. This provides for the child the freedom to use any language they may have at their disposal at the time, and does not constrain the child in any way to matching the language which was used by the teacher.

The value of reading aloud to a child

Research has presented unequivocal evidence of the cognitive, linguistic and emotional value of reading aloud to children. For example, it has been found that frequent exposure to book reading may positively impact children's later mathematics and reading development (Barnes and Puccioni 2017; Birckmayer et al 2009).

Reading aloud to children helps develop their language, whether they are native speakers of the language of the book or not. Snow and Ninio (1992) observe how much language development (for children being read to in their first language) occurs through adult-child book reading, especially when the same book is repeated a few times. They conclude that book reading may be "the ideal routine for language learning".

Providing daily teacher "read-alouds" for first graders has been found to have beneficial effects. Students who experience frequent "read-alouds" spend more time silently reading to themselves, and seem to enjoy silent reading more, than children who do not experience read-alouds (Pegg and Bartelheim 2011).

A useful idea is to allow the child to take a picture book home for their parents to read to them, or simply for them to look at and enjoy the pictures. This is important for the silent child: by doing this we create a link between the child's familiar home space and the less familiar school space. If the child feels completely safe at home but not safe at school, creating a link between home and school might in effect allow some of that feeling of safety to flow over into the school setting. Winnicott (1957) talks of the "transitional object" as a connection, or link, in tangible form, between the child's home and the outside world.

Reading aloud to the child is also a way to strengthen the bond between the teacher and the child. It provides a dimension of "shared common ground" (Danon-Boileau 2001) for the child: the teacher sits next to rather than opposite the child, so that the story is experienced by both of them together, in a parallel seated situation. The teacher can then let the child hold the book, or turn the pages, thereby inviting the child to become a more active participant in the experience.

However it is very important not to allow the sessions to be dominated by the teacher using all the therapy time in reading to the child. This would, of course, offer opportunities for the child to hear language, and thereby to experience much language input; we have seen above how reading to children is a vital part of education. However, the aim in this programme is to encourage communicative interaction, and to help the child develop a more active role in this communication. Reading to a child can put the child in a passive situation, in which they do not play any interactive role. The benefit of reading aloud to a child certainly plays a part in the child's exposure to language input and to literacy, but cannot be sufficient for the purposes of helping the silent child to overcome their silence. The pretend play, and the use of narrative emerging from that play, are the main components of the StoryFrames programme.

The box below lays out a few suggestions for reading aloud to children. These are useful ways to use picture books with all children, and are not specific in any way to the StoryFrames programme. This is probably very familiar to early years' teachers, but will be useful for any student teacher, social worker, or parent, who may wish to run this programme.

Ways to read aloud to young children using picture books

When reading aloud to young children, there are several things we can do to enhance the experience. Through reading picture books in a variety of ways, we can instil in young children a feeling of love and fascination for books, which will be of lasting value to them throughout their lives. Reading aloud to children, using illustrated books, can be interesting and fun, even for the youngest children, and even for children who do not understand the language used in the book.

- **Where to sit:** When reading aloud, sit next to the child instead of opposite the child. This ensures that you both have the same (literal) point of view; the child sees exactly what you see. In addition the child can follow your pointing finger, and this introduces the concept of the direction of print: which side of the page we start reading from, in which direction the line continues, how we drop down to the next line and in which order we turn the pages.

- **When and how to introduce the picture books to the child:** Before you start the actual reading, you can introduce various interesting things about the book itself. Talk about the cover, its pictures and colours. Talk about the title of the book and explain that a title is the name of the book, just as every child has a name. Page through a few pages of the book without reading, and point out some pictures and characters, making 'pondering' comments such as "I wonder who this is?" or "I wonder why the dog is doing that? Let's read and see."

- **Allow the child to hold the book and turn the pages:** This provides for the child a sense of ownership and active participation in the reading, instead of being a passive listener.

- **Discussion and comment:** You can, of course, read the book straight through without stopping, but you can also stop at any stage before, during and after the reading for some discussion. Discuss the pictures, the events, the characters, and the feelings which the characters might feel. If something interesting happens in the story, you can comment: "That is so interesting/sad/wonderful!" or " I really like the way she…" With older children, and children who have sufficient language to deal with this kind of discussion, you can ask "what would you do if that was you?" [NOTE: In the StoryFrames programme such a question would only be asked towards the end of the programme. See the section on 'Asking questions' in Chapter 10 below.]

- **Use varied language:** to talk about what *has* happened (past tense) and what *might* happen (future and conditional tenses). Be careful not to ask too many questions; we do not want the child to feel that a response is demanded. Rather use a pondering attitude: "I wonder what will happen next! Let's think what will happen… I wonder what the boy will decide to do, let's read on, and see."

- Using age-appropriate vocabulary, you can talk with the child about **who the characters are** and **what they might do or feel.** This serves to model the **vocabulary of feelings:** "If this happened to me I would be/ I would feel…"

- Using the language of cause and effect (why, because) can help develop the child's language beyond simple sentences. "I wonder why…." or "The boy might decide to… because he is feeling….."

- **Use props:** a fun way to make a story come to life is to prepare props which represent the character and the objects in the story. For example, in the story of Goldilocks and the three bears, you could use a doll, teddies and toy furniture. You and the child can then act out the story, both during the reading and after. This helps the child to be an active participant in the story. The use of props is very helpful for a child who is new to the language and may not understand the story.

- **Frequency:** make reading aloud a regular activity. Many research studies have shown how regular reading aloud to children helps them to learn to read, as well as helping them to develop language and concentration.

- **Read the same book several times:** this is a very effective way to consolidate the language of the book in the child's mind. The first reading is when we hear what happens in the story and we encounter the vocabulary; on the second reading we start to think about the characters; on the third reading the child remembers the story and starts to predict what will happen when you turn the page, and the last reading sets the child up to retell the entire story independently.

- **Use books with songs and rhymes:** Some books have short, rhyming texts which may also have been set to music. Many of these are available on YouTube. These books do not necessarily tell a story with a plot, but rather present repeated examples of a category: for example, books showing several types of vehicle, each one with a different shape, size or colour; or books with a different animal on each page. Many children begin to sing along very early on in their language development.

- **Summing up:** You can finish reading the book with comments such as "I liked that story, because…" or "I liked this character best because…" or "…It is a sad/ happy/ funny story, isn't it?" By summing up in this way we introduce the child to *meta-cognitive concepts*: thinking about thinking, thinking about our experiences, and how to put thinking into words.

The transcript below is of a session in which a picture book was read to Child B in the original research project:

CHILD B	[The child picks up a rhyming book which has a picture of a different animal on each page; the teacher has used this specific book during two previous sessions and the child has clearly enjoyed it. The book has a repetitive sentence structure and the same rhyming sentence on every page (Carle 1969)]
	We read that book every day!
	[He starts singing along with the teacher, using full sentences exactly as they have been read to him; the use of the tune and the rhythm seem to help him to recall the complete sentences even though he does not yet have much spoken language in English.]
	[The teacher shows him a boxed set of picture cards which present the same animals, but which are slightly different in posture, size and colour from those in the book]
CHILD B	[He starts to compare the loose pictures to those in the book]
	Look at this one, is sitting down, so that one is not sitting down.
	[Note the use of complete sentences here; at that stage in the programme this child was just beginning to use such sentences]
CHILD B	That one is laughing and this one is not laughing
	[The teacher then puts out all the cards in a line, from left to right, but not in the sequence which matches the pictures in the book. Child B spontaneously re-arranges them to match the sequence in the book.]

***

CHAPTER 6

Implementing the StoryFrames programme

The StoryFrames acronym

The name of the programme serves as a mnemonic to help us remember the stages and strategies used.

Story	The use of narrative structure
F	Feelings
R	Repeating
A	Adding (words and phrases)
M	Modelling (of narrative structure)
E	Expanding
S	Space (safety and seclusion)

The first part of the title ("Story") refers to the main element used: narrative, or stories, as discussed in Chapter Five above.

The second part of the title, comprising the letters F, R, A, M and E, is an acronym for the five stages through which we progress, and the strategies used in each stage while carrying out the programme. The final S in the title refers to the dedicated space in which the programme takes place.

These six crucial "ingredients" are what make this programme somewhat different from more traditional programmes of speech and language therapy and of second language teaching.

The importance of a carefully planned sequential programme emerges in the writings of Bruner (1986). Bruner suggests that children learn tasks through the adult or teacher providing a "scaffold", that is, a graded and progressive supporting structure, to enable the child to pass through the stages of learning.

In the StoryFrames programme, the stages are presented sequentially: we start at the beginning. However, it is important to note that as the programme progresses, it will often be beneficial to return to earlier strategies and activities, and we often use more than one strategy in one session. This is because the social, cognitive and linguistic skills involved in the creating and telling of a narrative interact with each other.

A return to a previous level of the scaffold might sometimes be necessary. For example, if a child is thinking about a situation which is complex socially, they may revert to using more basic language. If the context of the story is cognitively complex, the child may revert to a less socially interactive mode. If the story the child is playing out is emotionally difficult, they child may repeat the same play sequence over and over, and even if the child has started to speak, they may revert for a while to total silence. The teacher should respond flexibly to the child, applying strategies which seem to tie in with the child's linguistic and emotional needs of the moment.

It is important to stress the need for flexibility in the work being done here: no rigid sequence of activities will ever be able to replicate the sequence of a child's social, cognitive and language development as it naturally unfolds. The feedback loops and causal connections between these three areas of development are too inter-related and inter-dependent. The use of the five techniques are presented here conceptually as "stages" or "steps" in that it is not recommended to begin working with a silent child by using a later stage when the child is not ready for this, but we always have the option to go back a stage or two and then forward again. The main thing is to be careful not to push the child into an advanced stage before they are ready.

***

CHAPTER 7

S is for Safe Secluded Space

The first thing to consider when running the StoryFrames programme is the space in which we carry out the sessions. The S in the programme's name stands for Safe Secluded Space. Danon-Boileau (2001) talks of the provision of a "shared space" as a way of supporting children emotionally. This is a crucial component in the success of the programme.

These children are often overwhelmed by the social environment of school: many children talking at once, questions being asked which the child cannot even understand, looking on while other people do new and different things, and the feeling of having arrived in a place where everything is different, and none of the previously familiar events or objects or people or sounds are present (Hoffman 2008).

With some children, we may observe in their posture and facial features an aspect of immobility. In this case, their silence is not only the silence of not speaking, but a kind of 'frozen' silence of a person who seems fearful of drawing attention to themselves in any way. This is the 'freeze' defence mechanism, which may be activated if the defence mechanisms of 'fight or flight' are not an option (Thompson et al 2014). One of the children in the original research project, Child A, would freeze if anyone walked past the place where we were having our sessions, and remain completely immobile until the person had walked away.

The space is especially important for a child who is a refugee for social or economic reasons, who has suffered the trauma of dislocation and perhaps danger to life. For such a child, the experience of being in a safe, secluded and unchanging space, week after week, with the same toys and the same trusted teacher, is healing in itself. For this reason, it is important that the sessions take place in the same physical place throughout the entire programme.

In the Montessori education philosophy, the structure of the physical environment is seen "as another teacher" (Le Courtois et al 2023): the very way in which the space is constructed and arranged sends a clear message to the child. In the case of the StoryFrames programme, the message is that this is a place of calm, quiet and retreat, a place of predictability, where each session will be similar to the last. This provides the assurance of a safe present which can unfold into a safe future. It is this atmosphere which is a significant factor in enabling these children to emerge from their silence. In providing a "shared space" which is dedicated only to the child and the trusted teacher or therapist, we provide a haven of seclusion, quiet and safety. The emotional support provided in this way is crucial in reducing the anxieties of the silent child.

This space should be away from the busy classroom, ideally in a quiet place where there are no passers-by. It might be quite a challenge to create such a space in a busy school, which usually does not have either spare space or the funding for special equipment. In the kindergarten where the original research was carried out there was an unused space at the end of a corridor, in which the teachers had placed an old four-poster double bed. This proved to be an ideal hideaway, as the teachers had draped saris over the posts, making the space inside partially hidden from passers-by. With tiny battery-powered tealights and soft cushions, it became a most attractive and welcoming place for children to feel secluded and safe. We referred to it as "the cave".

It is also possible, if no other space is to be found, to achieve this feeling of seclusion by curtaining off a corner of a classroom, using curtains suspended from the ceiling, and putting big cushions on the floor inside the space. Elizabeth Jarman provides practical ideas as to how to create such a space (Jarman 2023).

How we position ourselves in the space where the sessions take place is also important. Danon-Boileau (2001) recommends sitting next to, rather than opposite the child, so that the teacher and child share the same point of view. Sitting next to the child gives a clear message that the teacher is present, sharing the space and following the action, even if not intervening. This ensures that the child experiences the interaction as "joint attention." Sitting opposite each other can lead to the teacher needing to point to the toys to refer to them, and some young children with developmental delay have difficulty following a pointing finger and knowing that the teacher is referring to the thing being pointed to. For these reasons, sitting next to the child is important.

For children having to learn in a language which is not their home language, school must feel very strange and unfamiliar. One way to help such a child feel more comfortable is to keep in the therapy space some objects or books from their home language and culture. The child's parents can be invited to bring a traditional costume from home, or a picture book or photographs showing where the family lived previously. The drapes which are used to cover the therapy space can also be something typical of the country of origin of the child.

In the original research programme, the two participating children were always very willing, and even excited, to "go play in the cave." Even after the programme had ended, and the teacher was still visiting the school on occasion, they would come up to her to ask if they could go to the cave with her and play.

Once the child has become a more confident speaker, we can gradually reduce the level of seclusion, perhaps by opening or even removing the drapes. Later we can move the sessions closer to the classroom. The aim is to gradually expose the child, in small steps, to the use of language in the presence of other people.

***

CHAPTER 8

F is for Feelings

The concept of Feelings here refers to the basic principle, which is carried throughout the programme, of creating an atmosphere in which the child does not feel pressured to speak, or to behave in any required manner. The aim is for the child to feel safe and relaxed during the sessions.

The programme is based on an assumption that a significant cause for the silence of many of these children is an emotional response to changes in the child's life: the physical move to a new place, the loss of their previous community which was familiar and in which people spoke their language, and the confusion of going to a new school where the child cannot understand what is being said, or ask for what they need.

The one-to-one nature of the StoryFrames programme, with its non-critical acceptance of whatever the child does, is designed to provide the silent and isolated child with a feeling of emotional safety, and a situation in which it might be safe to speak. Barbara Frederickson (2002) reminds us of the importance of positive emotions in encouraging communication: such emotions enable the child to feel more willing to engage with another person, to be attentive to another person, and therefore to be more likely to listen to and retain the language being used by the other person. We use the shared space to work towards developing an emotional connection between the teacher and the silent child, to "create and sustain emotional bonds" between the storyteller and the listener (Fivush 2022).

Winnicott's term "a holding environment" (1957, 2018) describes what the experience of the sessions needs to represent for the child. Winnicott writes extensively about the feeling of safety which parents provide, and which sets the foundation of a lasting feeling of security and attachment in children. The StoryFrames programme is geared towards providing such a feeling of safety and continuity, as a result of the calm, accepting, non-demanding attitude of the teacher, as well as the continuity provided by having the same teacher with the same toys in the same place, week after week.

A balance is struck between the teacher's quiet observation of the child at play, and an overly interventionist attitude. The teacher does not have to be completely silent; a sympathetic sigh, a word or two, are of course acceptable, as long as the teacher is following the child's lead in the play and not making suggestions or requests or demands. One way to describe the feeling we project towards the child is encompassed in the words of Rogers (1956) as "unconditional positive regard".

This is not to say that the teacher is a non-involved or passive observer of the child's play. The teacher does respond, but strictly in a way which suggests to the child that their feelings, whatever they may be, are being accepted and respected. The concept of "witnessing" is useful here. The response of the adult provides a consistent calm presence, attentively watching the play, and accepting what the child presents. There is no analysis of the feelings on the part of the teacher: as I have said above, this programme is not play therapy.

Another aspect which falls under the heading of "Feelings" is the 'feeling of agency.' By 'agency', we mean the feeling one has when one has control over the events around us, and over the actions we choose to carry out. If we have a sense of agency, we can make choices and decisions to influence what happens to us, and feel that we can, in some way, have an impact on the world.

We can only imagine the effect on a young child of a move to a new country, where people do not speak your language. In addition, the trauma of the refugee experience could certainly rupture a child's sense of agency, and the world might now look to be a place where nothing is under control, where consequences are random, and where safety is lost. If we try to see the world through the child's eyes, we might speculate that for such a child the only agency remaining to them is the choice to remain silent (Granger 2004).

It is of course possible that initially the child might feel strange being the sole focus of the teacher's attention. The child might suddenly notice "the visibility of oneself to another" (Reddy 2008 p 126) and find this uncomfortable, or threatening. For this reason, the intensity and pace of attention need to be carefully managed by the teacher: not too much, not too little. The aim is not to intrude in the pretend play but to simply be a calm presence. Danon-Boileau (2001) says a good principle to adhere to in these sessions is always to listen more than you talk. The teacher indicates, through facial expression, gesture, and encouraging sounds, that they are listening, but does not impose, comment, or suggest.

Another important aspect of Feelings is creating for the child the feeling that their interests and needs are seen as worthy of notice and respect. Reddy refers to "attentional coordination" as one of the vital aspects in the development and successful attainment of dialogue and communication: "...the ability to know when someone is attending to you and to co-ordinate your attention with the other's to a third thing." (Reddy 2008 p 71).

The very presence of another person, witnessing the child's pretend play, is therapeutic in itself, according to Danon-Boileau (2001). The child who is silent and also socially isolated will seldom have, at the new school, the experience of participating in shared attentional coordination with another person to a toy, an activity or an event. The presence of another person who can provide such an experience of attentional coordination is invaluable in building the child's feeling that they might share their thoughts with another person.

Reddy (2008 p 83) uses the phrase "the magic that happens when someone who isn't expecting to be heard is heard" and this is indeed what takes place in the StoryFrames programme: the child seems to quickly realise that this particular teacher is someone who is not only interested in what they were doing, but will make no demands on them to speak, or to be or do anything other than what they want to be or do. This appears to free the child from the anxiety which seems to be so much part of their daily experience at school. They begin to play freely, and a short while after that, to use their voice.

As we have said, in this initial pretend play stage there is no expectation at all for spoken language from the child. The teacher pays careful attention to the play, so that the child can see that the teacher is interested, but the teacher does not indicate that speech is expected. The teacher does not direct or join in the play in any way. This in itself takes the pressure off the child and promotes the child's feeling of being in a calm, undemanding place. The teacher accepts calmly and unconditionally the pretend play of the child. Any assumptions about the feelings of the child are not commented on or responded to in any way which might suggest a reaction, either positive or negative.

In the later stages of the programme, once the child has started to use language to tell their story, the teacher may introduce some words for specific feelings, and model the use of these words so that the child can learn to name their feelings, but in these initial stages this is avoided. It is important not to over-interpret (e.g. "that is so scary!" or "that is terrible".) In general the response should be more one of observation than of interpretation.

The feelings of the teacher working with a silent child

This section of the programme deals with feelings. Thus far we have discussed extensively the feelings that might have led the child to a position of silence in the first place, the feelings the child might have as a result of their social isolation, and the feelings the child might experience while taking part in the programme. However, it is also important to think about the feelings of the teacher who is running this kind of programme.

It is not comfortable for anyone to be in the presence of someone who does not notice us, and who does not even make non-verbal attempts to communicate. Once the child in the programme begins to play, it is also difficult to hear children sometimes demonstrating ideas and situations which are violent and frightening, and to stay calm without responding with alarm. The child's unspoken but often clearly expressed feelings come through in their pretend play, and later, in the narratives they tell. The natural response of the teacher is to find out more and to try to help. The fact that the teacher is the person who is supposed to 'fix' this situation makes our feelings even more confusing.

As teachers and therapists, we are often anxious about doing the right thing, and about doing enough for the children in our care. This is especially the case in working with silent children, because we often have no way of knowing if, and how, they are responding to our efforts. They may provide little or no feedback.

It will sometimes seem strange and unfeeling to make no response at all to some of the events in the pretend play. So, for example, if the child in play shows something that is painful, we might, in this "Feelings" stage of the programme, nod, or show in our facial expressive an appropriate response. Or we might even use a sound or gesture: we might say "ow!" if something looks painful, or if something seems scary we might say "oh my goodness!" Or we might say nothing at all, but continue to watch attentively. For those of us who are accustomed to taking an active teaching role, and to engage fully with each child, working with the silent child feels very different. We are being asked to hold back, not to respond, and not to (overtly) provide help. This goes against all our training.

We will all have feelings about the child's silence: empathy, and concern about whether we are helping. We will respond to the child's feelings: sometimes we will feel touched, sometimes worried, sometimes threatened by this silence which is our responsibility to 'solve'. We as teachers and speech and language therapists carry a heavy burden in trying to help the child to feel comfortable, secure, and confident. We have no way of knowing, initially, if our intervention is helping or hindering. It is very helpful, if at all possible, for a person running this programme to be in touch with other people who are also running the programme, so as to discuss and compare ideas and feelings.

The hardest feeling to contemplate might be the feeling that the child has a right to remain silent, and that this is a justifiable choice being made, even if a choice made in very difficult circumstances. The child, by choosing not to communicate, may be expressing their sense of agency in the only way available to them at the time.

As teachers and therapists, everything we do, all our experience and all our training, has led us in the direction of intervention: we are here to help, to support, to show how. In the case of the silent child, we might just have to take a back seat for a while.

***

In summary, this early stage of the programme is carefully designed to provide for the silent child an experience of feeling safe in the presence of another's calm and non-judgemental attention. The feelings which we try to emit in this stage are of acceptance, encouragement, respect and joint attention. The feeling of predictability which we create through maintaining this consistent attitude might provide for the child their first pleasant or positive emotion within the new school space.

***

CHAPTER 9

R is for Repeating

The second stage of this programme is repeating. Here, 'Repeating' refers to two rather different concepts:

- The strategy of repetition by the teacher of the child's sounds or words
- The tendency of many children to repeat the same pretend play, week after week

Repetition of the child's words or sounds by the teacher

Once the child starts to feel relaxed in the space, they usually begin spontaneously to make sounds to accompany their stories. In this early stage of the programme, these are usually sound effects ("Pow!!" "Whoosh!" or "Grrr...") rather than words. Often in these sessions, the child becomes lost in play, and seems to forget that we are there.

However, the moment in which the child begins to make sounds marks a significant step forward: the child is relaxing *and voicing* in the presence of another person. This is often the first time the silent child has used their voice at all in the school space.

At this stage, the teacher begins to repeat the sounds that the child is making. This repetition is a kind of imitation. Imitation in this sense is "a means of making contact in the absence of any common language...it seems to establish something shared, some common ground... a way in which both people... can touch each other psychologically." (Reddy 2008)

The theoretical motivation behind imitation of the child by the teacher can be seen in a very well-established programme which uses imitation: Intensive Interaction (Caldwell 2002). In this programme, which has been successfully used with non-verbal children who have severe developmental delay or are on the autistic spectrum, the teacher or therapist uses imitation of the child's movements or physical stance in order to create common psychological ground with the child.

Nadel (2002) suggests that imitation is a kind of compliment to the person being imitated; it shows that the imitator is interested in what the child is doing, and accepts that whatever the child does, thinks or feels is of value to the person imitating. It is not done in any sense of mimicry or flattery, but with the intention of confirming that the teacher values, and is attending to, whatever feelings or ideas the child is bringing to the session.

This idea is also found in the writing of Zeedyk (2006) who views imitation in the sense of creating a feeling of intimacy; the person who imitates is playing close attention to the person being imitated. The child is reassured of being seen and heard in spite of not yet using words. The child can then begin to build an identity of a person who exists and acts in this new school environment; in other words, the child begins to develop a sense of agency, or an "idea of me" (Lewis 1999).

It is this *use of voice itself*, and not whether or not the child is using words, which is a big step forward for these silent children. For the very shy and quiet child, just making a sound or a noise can be a challenge, as it draws attention to them, which they may be trying to avoid.

In most cases, after this stage has been reached, the children begin shortly afterwards, quite spontaneously, to use words, or even short sentences. Here again the strategy of repetition is used, and the teacher simply repeats verbatim the words that the child has said. At this stage we do not expand on the child's words by creating phrases or sentences, and we do not ask questions. We are not trying to model any language structure, but rather simply to acknowledge that the child has said something and that we have heard it.

Here is a transcript from a session with Child B in which the teacher uses repetition of what the child has just said, in order to indicate that she is listening with interest to his story:

Speaker	Transcript	Strategy
	[Child B takes three cows, one small, one medium and one big, and puts them in the river which the teacher has drawn for him on a post-it note.]	
CHILD B	Baby cow, Mommy cow, Daddy cow. The policeman put them in a river	
TEACHER	They're in a river	R: Repeating
CHILD B	And then jumping inside the river	
TEACHER	In the river	R: Repeating

Repetition by the child of their own pretend play

The other face of repetition in the programme is seen when we find that a child chooses the same toys over and over, and enacts the same scenes, session after session. It is as if the children are imitating themselves. In the original StoryFrames research project, the police cars and the fire engine were repeatedly used by Child B in pretend play about accidents or disasters. The miniature animals and furniture were repeatedly used by Child A throughout the programme.

In looking at the repetitive nature of the play of most of the children who have participated in this programme, it might seem that the amount of time spent on this repetitive activity is a waste of valuable therapy time, and that more progress could be made if the teacher would provide more varied or different input. After all, the child is playing with the same toys, making up what is often the same story, over and over.

However, not only is there no problem with this repetition, but it is in fact an important part of the process. The child is clearly enacting something that is important to them, and re-enacting it as many times as needed, in order to hold these ideas and feelings. Margaret Donaldson (1992) refers to the repeated sharing of activities over time: she talks of sharing space and time, and sharing "concerns and purposes" as part of the developmental process.

Danon-Boileau writes that "the fundamental problem of all communication lies in defining the common ground; ... [and] repetition [of previous games and actions] is an easy way of doing this" (Danon-Boileau 2001 p 15).

Reddy (2008 p 18) refers to "the engagement over time" in describing the value of doing things together, repeatedly, over an extended time. These repetitions are meaningful to the child. By accepting this repetition on the part of the child, the teacher is showing the child that these things are meaningful to the teacher too.

This is why it is important to use the same set of toys every week, and why the same toys should be presented in the same container, packed and organised in the same way each week. This repetition allows the child to "capitalize on shared memories of previous sessions - what was played with and said last time" (Danon-Boileau 2001). In this way the child can make an emotional link between past sessions and today's experiences, and thereby gain the feeling that life is predictable, and not subject to the shocks and changes that a child escaping from a war zone, or traumatized by the move to a new environment, might have experienced.

Having said that, on occasion the child does seem "stuck" in overly-repetitive play. It is difficult to provide hard and fast rules as to when to intervene in the repetition, and sometimes the teacher has to trust in their judgement and sensitively try to move the play on. Please see the topic "Adding a new object or toy" in the next chapter, for suggestions about when and how to move forward in this respect.

Staying with the theme of repetition, we can also read the same picture book several times, if it is one which the child seems to enjoy. In the original programme, Child B repeatedly requested that the teacher read to him from the same small selection of books. This is understandable, in that once a child has heard a book once, they are able to predict what comes next, which must provide some sense of consistency, control and safety. The children then often start to join in if there are repetitive phrases used in the story and in this way they begin to use the new language without the added burden of having to think about how to say what we want to say.

If we are using the StoryFrames programme with children who have a diagnosed speech or language delay, or children who stutter, this stage of repetition is very important, as it serves to confirm to the child that we have accepted and understood what they have said, no matter how they have said it or how long they have taken to say it. They seem to gain confidence from this, and to become willing to speak more often.

***

CHAPTER 10

A is for Adding

At this stage, in order to take the play and the stories to the next step, the teacher adds something new to the sessions. We do this by using two kinds of "adding" strategies:

- Adding *a new object* to the set of toys
- The teacher begins to *add new words*

Adding a new object or toy

Having stressed the value of letting the child repeat the same pretend play with the same tiny toys many times, and listen to the same book over and over, there does come a time when the child's play seems overly repetitive. A child might re-enact a car crash, or a fight between two characters, over and over, and seems to be "stuck" in this mode of pretend play. So although the basic principle is to accept whatever the child chooses to do in the sessions, there does come a time when we want to move things on a little.

In order to do this, we can introduce a new object or miniature toy. There is no hard-and-fast rule about when we decide to add a new toy or object; if we offer a novel toy and the child does not want it, we pack it away. This idea comes from the work of Danon-Boileau, who calls this technique "introducing a slight disturbance" (Danon-Boileau 2001 p 15). He shows how, in his work with non-verbal children, this new object can be a very useful strategy in leading to some kind of change in the atmosphere of a therapy session.

In order to do this, we keep hidden one or two additional miniature toys or objects. We produce the object as if by magic, and offer it to the child. If the child wants to take it, they will, and the new object will be incorporated into the pretend play, thereby moving it forward in some way. In this way a new idea or action can be subtly inserted into this repetitive play at a carefully judged time.

The new object could be any toy or small object: a feather, a toy car, a toy apple, or a shiny stone. The new object can be introduced with a phrase such as "and suddenly along came a..." or "suddenly there was a feather."

Introducing one additional item into the already-established and familiar process of the sessions to extend the story does not provoke any dramatic change. What we are adding here is quantitative but not qualitative. The timing of this, and being sensitive to the child's response, is important. The disturbance can either disrupt the play totally, or, if done sensitively, can be very effective in leading the child to new and more complex ideas.

Adding words

The other important change we can begin to introduce at this stage is actual words, as opposed to the sounds we have been imitating up to now. This is the first time in this programme when the child might possibly feel that there is something being imposed on them; something not of the child's own making or choice. At this stage the child might feel as if our words are intruding into their play.

For this reason, the teacher's use of speech during the sessions must be done very sensitively and gradually.

The intention at this stage of the programme is not to provide a language model for the child to learn, but rather to gradually introduce to the child a new idea: the idea that words and sentences can be used to describe and to remember their pretend play. So, for example, if the child has made two cars crash into each other, with the child making sounds such as "wham" or "crash", we can now say a very short sentence, describing the event. For example, "The two cars crashed".

We make sure that we are not adding our own ideas to the session, but simply describing what the child has chosen to do; whatever we say relates entirely to the pretend play of the child. In this way the words are not intrusive, but rather confirming of and relevant to the child's pretend play. In this respect, the StoryFrames programme is very different in concept and intention from theories of intensive comprehensible input (Krashen 1981) as described in Chapter One above, in which the teacher tries to provide as much variety as possible in the vocabulary and syntax being presented to the child as input.

The next transcript gives an example of adding words. Note that the strategy of Repetition from the previous stage continues to be used, as and when it is felt to be necessary. The earlier stages of the programme can be returned to at any time, and we do this frequently, even in more advanced stages of the programme.

In light of the fact that this transcript was recorded in the third session with this child, it is remarkable how much language she was able to produce, in spite of her having been silent for so many months. This can be seen as confirmation of the 'input' theories: she had clearly been absorbing language in her time in the classroom, even though she had not spoken at all. However the fact that she had internalised this amount of language, but still did not speak in the classroom or the playground, is also confirmation of the socio-cognitive view: Language is so much more than linguistic facility; as clearly stated by Lave and Wenger (1991) the child needs to learn to "negotiate meaning" in the new culture. This was something that this child was not yet ready to do.

Speaker	Transcript	Strategy
CHILD A	[Playing with the miniature gecko, turtle and frog. She has been repeating a story she had played during previous sessions, about the animals needing to sleep and not having a place to sleep] ... And the gecko was..... [she shows the gecko walking]	
TEACHER	And the gecko walked	A: Adding words
CHILD A	And the gecko said, where can I sleep? A bed...	
TEACHER	He needs a bed	R: Repeating A: Adding words
CHILD A	Here's a one. [she picks up the toy bunk bed] Ladder. [she picks up the ladder which connects the lower bunk bed to the upper bunk bed]	
TEACHER	Here's the ladder. Gecko said, where can I sleep?	R: Repeating A: Adding words
CHILD A	On that! [She picks up the miniature table and puts the gecko on the table]	
TEACHER	On the table. So you put the gecko on the table.	A: Adding words

Adding our own words in this way is a strategy whereby we become slightly more actively involved in the child's pretend play and storytelling. The use of language by the teacher in these sessions is expanded very gradually, in accordance with the thinking of Vygotsky (1978) who describes how the mediator develops the child's skills step by step, by always supporting the child to move just that one step further than what the child can already do on their own. In Vygotsky's words, "what the child is able to do in collaboration today he will be able to do independently tomorrow" (Vygotsky 1978 p 211). The idea is echoed in Bruner's concept of "scaffolding" (Bruner 1986).

The theories of Feuerstein (2015) and of Vygotsky (1978) show us that merely providing opportunities for pretend play and narrative in a safe space is not enough. The benefits of pretend play will be felt only through the active and intentional intervention of a teacher who deliberately mediates putting play into language. What we are introducing at this stage is not a linguistic structure, but rather the idea that the pretend play can be described in language, and that two people can together listen to and produce this language.

How do we choose what to say and which words to add?

It is important at this stage for the teacher to use very short and simple sentences, to limit the amount of speaking and not to describe every move the child makes, so as not to interrupt the child's absorption in their play.

It is also critically important at this stage to take great care that the child does not feel as if we are trying to tell them what they should have, or could have, said or done. We are simply acknowledging that the child is in the presence of another person; a person who is interested in what is happening, and in what the child is doing, and who can put those actions into words.

The words we introduce could relate to something the child *might* have said, based on the pretend play. In other words, we add words to *describe* something we see taking place in the child's pretend play. On occasion a teacher gets it wrong, and the child might notice this. Sometimes they respond with a quick sharp glance which tells us we have misunderstood. On other occasions, after describing in a sentence what the teacher has seen in the pretend play, the child suddenly looks up and meets their eye, which signals to the teacher that they have understood correctly, and that the words said were acceptable to and understood by the child. The child in this way indicates an awareness of the teacher's intention, and sends a clear communicative message. This communicative gaze towards the teacher is significant, as it is a non-verbal communication and not a withdrawal from communication. It marks a tiny step towards the child's beginning to emerge from the Silent Period, and the start of an ability to negotiate meaning (Wenger 1998). Daniel Stern (2004) talks of such changes as "now moments": the moment in which the relationship between two people is transformed.

Here is an example of such an occasion in which the therapist tries to participate in a story by adding words, but clearly gets it wrong:

Speaker	Transcript	Strategy
CHILD B	[The child has been telling the teacher about a time when something fell on his brother's toe and it hurt; the teacher does not completely understand what he has been saying so makes a guess, in an attempt at continuing his story]	
TEACHER	Once upon a time, your brother was playing and something fell on his toe.	A: Adding words
CHILD B	[Correcting the teacher's misunderstanding] All the cars did!	
TEACHER	All the cars dropped on his toe. It was sore.	A: Adding words
CHILD B	[Correcting the misunderstanding again] No! When he was sleeping in his bed he want to come to my bed so I said: No you can't!	[Typical narrative style of children around 3 years old; disconnected topics]
TEACHER	[The teacher is by this stage not sure whether this event is linked to the sore toe, but tries to follow the child's lead] Your brother was sleeping in his bed and he said, please can I sleep in your bed, and you said: No you can't!	R: Repeating
CHILD B	Now can I play with cars? [They move immediately to playing with cars. The teacher, realising she has not grasped what the child was trying to say, follows his lead and abandons the topic]	Following the child's lead at all times

In fact, this kind of "misunderstanding" is not a difficulty; it is rather a fact of everyday communication between two people. In any conversation, the meaning one person is trying to present to another often does need clarification.

Clarification of misunderstandings requires a sense of agency which enables one person to explain to another that they have misunderstood what they were trying to convey. The ability of a child to use clarification in the above transcript is not yet language-based, but he clearly has his own ideas as to what he is trying to put over, and this is a positive indication of a sense of agency in this child. It is this kind of change in the interaction between the teacher and the silent child which the StoryFrames programme aims to achieve. There is a growing feeling of, in the terms used by Smuts (2001) "presence" and "mutuality".

Of course, our use of words at this stage also serves a linguistic purpose: to introduce to the child a small vocabulary of words, and a small selection of grammatical structures, which are appropriate to their story. And even if this is not our primary aim, these words are likely to be relevant and interesting to the child because they emerge from their own story, and may therefore be remembered and used when the child next tells a story.

As we have seen, there is always the option of going back to an earlier strategy in the StoryFrames programme. The strategy of Repeating becomes useful once again here: once the child begins to speak and begins to tell a narrative, we can not only add new words but add the repetition of a more complete narrative: not our own ideas, of course, but the narrative which we understand that they are telling us. In this way, we are following the child's lead, and we are showing that we have heard, understood and valued their story. In the words of Engel (2016) we can, in this way, "amplify their voices."

Asking questions

Questions can be felt as intrusive, and in principle, at this stage, the programme is focused on accepting the child's play without making suggestions or asking questions. However, sometimes a question is unavoidable. For example, a child might indicate that they are searching for a toy which is not in the set, or that they need some kind of background landscape for their story. A question asked at this time might be something like "Do you want me to draw a river?" The child who does not wish to speak can simply nod or shake their head to reply. This is called a "closed question": a question with a limited range of possible answers, for example, yes or no. The question must relate to something which has just been done in the pretend play.

If we ask a closed question but the child does not answer the question in any way, we can then answer it ourselves, using yes or no, and perhaps adding a word or phrase. For example: we can ask a closed question such as "Is he sleeping?" and we can answer it ourselves, if the child does not, by saying "Yes, he is sleeping", or "No, he is not sleeping." Through repeated exposure to this kind of closed question the child might begin to feel comfortable, and not threatened, when being asked questions, and the questions might later become useful in demonstrating more complex language.

Here is a transcript from a session with Child B, showing how the teacher begins Adding words, while also using Repeating, and then uses a yes/no (closed) question.

Speaker	Transcript	Strategy
CHILD B	[Child B has chosen three cows of different sizes. He names them Baby, Mommy cow, Daddy cow] The policeman put them in the river [he is using the picture of a river which the teacher had drawn previously]	
TEACHER	They're all in the river	R: Repeating
CHILD B	I need a policeman!	
TEACHER	[The teacher gives the child the police car and a bus. He puts the car and the bus in the river]	
CHILD B	I put them all in the river	
TEACHER	And they're swimming in the river	R: Repeating A: Adding words
CHILD B	And then jumping inside the river	
TEACHER	In the river	R: Repeating
CHILD B	Did you bring a shark?	
TEACHER	I didn't bring a shark. Do you want one in the river?	Yes/no question
CHILD B	Yes!	
TEACHER	I can draw one [The teacher draws a shark on a post-it note]	
CHILD B	He eat them up and they all go [unintelligible] and they got bleed on themself [sic]	
TEACHER	They're all bleeding!	A: Adding words

When using a picture book, there is often plenty of opportunity to use closed questions. For example, if the story says that the dog went into the house, we can ask "Did he go in the garden?" (No) "Did he go in a car?" (No) "Did he go in the house?" (Yes). The teacher can then provide the answer, adding words in order to present a full sentence: "Yes, he went in the house." This method of using closed questions, and questions to which we are sure the child knows the answer, appears in the TPRS programme to teach a second language (see Chapter Three above) and is not only an effective way of developing language skills, but also a source of fun for most children, who may find our questions ridiculously silly; they may enjoy having a laugh at our seeming confusion, when the answer is so obvious.

***

CHAPTER 11

M is for Modelling

After a few sessions in which the child has used the toys in pretend play, and the teacher has gained the trust of the child through repetition of their words, and through adding words or phrases, the next step can be taken. This is where we begin modelling the telling of a story, which is based on the child's pretend play.

Young children learn new skills naturally by modelling what other people in their surroundings are doing (Bandura 1977). A child who may not yet have been on a slide will watch other children and mimic them, and in this way learn how to use playground equipment. Children are often able to mimic songs and performances which they have seen and heard on television. The modelling of a linguistic structure is somewhat more complicated, but by using small steps and gradually building up towards more complex forms, this can be achieved.

The modelling stage of the StoryFrames programme can be introduced once the teacher feels relatively sure that the child is relaxed during the sessions, enjoys the pretend play, feels comfortable with the teacher adding words and is listening with enjoyment to the picture books. The teacher now begins to model the structure of a story.

A brief summary of some of the aspects of mature Story Grammar (Stein and Glenn 1979) is useful at this point. A typical story will include some or all of the following:

- An opening phrase (for example, "once upon a time", or "a long time ago")
- Characters
- A place where the action occurs
- A time when the action occurs
- An action which is carried out by a character
- The motivations of the characters: what they wish for, and why.
- A problem which might arise (the plot of the story)
- The feelings of the characters if they are met with the problem
- An attempt at a solution (making a plan)
- A consequence: finding a solution and putting things right
- The feelings of the characters once the solution is attempted or found
- An ending phrase (for example, The End)
- Usually the stories follow a logical time sequence of cause and effect.

As we have said, younger children might include only a few of these items, and as children develop and grow, their stories come to include many or all of the above.

We begin the modelling of the story structure by introducing phrases which relate to the actual activity of story-telling; we deliberately use the word "story" in order to introduce the topic to the child. For example, the teacher might say "Let's get the toys out of the box, and we can tell a story." We can use similar language when reading a picture book. For example, "I am going to read you this story" or "This is a story about a rabbit".

Some children enjoy it when we mention their name: "This is a story told by..." [child's name] or "This is [child's name]'s story." In this way we are ascribing agency and authorship to the child.

When beginning the story, we can use a traditional story introduction such as "One day..." or "Once there was..." or "Once upon a time..." Most children are accustomed to listening to children's stories being read to them at school, so these opening statements would be familiar to them.

We then very briefly summarise the story which we have just seen in the child's pretend play. For example, "One day, the car was driving very quickly and he crashed. Then the policeman came and he fixed the car." Or "Once upon a time there was a turtle, and he did not have a place to sleep. He found a bed and he went to sleep."

At the end of the story, the teacher can use a suitable phrase for story endings, for example "And that was your story!" or the more traditional "The end."

The concept of providing a model to introduce to the child the structure of a story brings us back to the socio-cultural theory of Lave and Wenger (1991) who use the term "improvised practice" for the step-by-step nature of learning through society: the child is offered a scaffold, or support, (Bruner 1986) through being provided with a model of story structure; the child is then offered multiple opportunities to practice by telling the stories of their own pretend play, over time, in a non-judgemental setting.

Through this kind of "apprenticeship" in storytelling, the child gradually learns how to "participate in the social world of the classroom" (Lave and Wenger 1991 p 43). This idea is similarly expressed by Sfard who conceptualises learning as "a process of becoming a member of a certain community" (Sfard 1998 p. 6) – in this case a community of children who interact with each other.

The following transcript is of a story told by Child B after the teacher has modelled the use of an opening phrase for a story. Once the story has started, the teacher adds, at times, additional events in the sequence of the story, always attempting to stick to the child's pretend play.

Speaker	Transcript	Strategy
	[The child is playing with the train]	
TEACHER	Once upon a time a train went into the station ….	M: Modelling opening phrase for a story
CHILD B	[The child picks up on the narrative style and continues the story] And the train can go all the way into the tunnel. [The child covers the train with a cloth to make a tunnel]	
TEACHER	And he said, Help, it's so dark in this tunnel!	A: Adding words M: Modelling story structure (sequence of events)
CHILD B	[Gaze shift towards the teacher, to make a request] We need a river!	Child showing social use of language: making a request
TEACHER	[The teacher gives the child a drawing of a river on a post-it note. The child makes the train fall into the river] Splash! They all fell into the river	A: Adding M: Modelling story structure (sequence of events)
CHILD B	[The child repeats the action of the train being covered with a cloth several times] And this one can go all the way back into the tunnel	
TEACHER	All the way back into the tunnel	R: Repeating
CHILD B	[The child makes the train fall over] And he was broken!	
TEACHER	The end.	M: Modelling story ending

We see in the above transcript how this child, whose narratives in the early sessions were a collection of loosely connected ideas, and sometimes just a random series of unconnected events, is now moving towards a more mature Story Grammar, where the sequential parts of the narrative relate to a single consistent theme.

Once several stories have been elicited using the modelling of story structure as a prompt for the child, we can move on to a stage where the child can tell a story independently, in response to an explicit invitation to tell a story. However, in our desire to elicit a story from the child we need to be careful never to instruct the child to tell the story; instead, our invitation to tell a story serves as a 'nudge' to lead the child towards a stage where they can tell a full story on their own.

The next transcript is from a session with Child A showing an example of the teacher using an invitation to the child to tell a story.

Speaker	Transcript	Strategy
TEACHER	[The teacher offers the child the box of toys] Do you want to tell me a story today?	M: Modelling story structure (explicit invitation to tell a story)
CHILD A	No! [This is the first time this child has been heard to say the word 'no' at school, possibly indicating a growing sense of agency. The teacher does not respond, but sits quietly]	
CHILD A	[The child picks up a miniature butterfly and makes it fly. She then, without further prompting, starts telling her story.] I can fly! I can fly! I can fly! I can fly!	
CHILD A	To the.... I'm flying! [She is using a slightly louder voice now]	The teacher remains silent, listening attentively, and not speaking, as the child has clearly taken on the role of narrator of her own story.
CHILD A	Higher and higher! [Using an even louder voice]	
CHILD A	And tumbled down [She makes the butterfly fall down]	
CHILD A	And couldn't fly. And he died. [Quiet voice]	The child has used a perfectly appropriate story ending phrase.

In the transcript above, the child's initial response of "no" to the teacher's invitation to tell a story is an important reminder never to rush the child. In this case, when we see how easily and quickly the child did actually tell a story without further prompting, we might speculate that her initial negative response came from the part of her identity as a silent person; perhaps she was then able to retrieve her growing sense of agency and tell her story, using her now louder and more confident voice.

Here is another example by the same child, in the same session: The teacher presents an invitation to tell a story. The child, without hesitation, and without the need for further prompts or invitations, picks up a toy and tells the entire story independently.

Speaker	Transcript	Strategy
TEACHER	Can you tell me another story?	M: Modelling story structure (Invitation to tell a story)
CHILD A	[Child A picks up a small dinosaur.] Then dinosaur want to grab [sic] out of the house.	
CHILD A	Oh! Oh! He can kick it and he can go out	
CHILD A	The she put... on the roof [The child puts the dinosaur on top of the box she is using to represent a house]	The child is now able to tell the full story, with no prompts from the teacher.
CHILD A	And then she was died.[sic]	

The next transcript from Child A (after six sessions) again shows her ability to tell an entire story, using aspects of Story Grammar: she spontaneously begins her story with "Once upon a time".

Speaker	Transcript	Strategy
	[The child is drawing pictures. She draws a tree]	
TEACHER	Do you want to tell me a story about the tree?	M: Modelling story structure (invitation to tell a story)
CHILD A	Once upon a time a tree was growing and growing and growing	Story Grammar: child uses traditional opening phrase for story
CHILD A	And then he tumbled down by a storm	Story Grammar: Use of "and then" indicates sequence in time
CHILD A	Then he died.	Story grammar: A consequence or outcome indicates the end of the story.

By this stage in the programme this child was speaking more freely during the sessions, and had started to speak a little in the classroom, albeit still in her quiet voice, to both teachers and children. Her sentences were becoming more grammatically accurate, and her vocabulary was growing.

This rapid language development supports the output theory of Swain (2001) which proposes that language expansion results from language use by the child: the more this child spoke in the StoryFrames sessions, the more developed her language became.

We can also surmise from the fact that she is now freely and happily telling complete stories during the sessions, that her feeling of agency has developed, and that she might now feel more free to interact with people outside of the sessions, thus gaining further opportunities for language output. As we have seen in the discussions of the theories around the Silent Period, no single causal factor is likely to be in operation on its own; social and linguistic development are inextricably linked to each other. These interactions are at play both in the causes of the silence, and in the emerging from the silence.

The teacher re-tells the story after it has been told by the child

Usually, by this stage in the programme, the child enjoys hearing their story repeated in full by the teacher; they know that their story has been attended to and understood, and they enjoy remembering what they did in their pretend play. What we do when we are retelling the child's story in full is to use brief but complete sentences to retell the story, and to use Story Grammar as much as is possible, based on the pretend play.

Sometimes a child will start to tell a story but not complete it, and may fall silent. This may be because they do not yet have the language to tell us everything they want to say. If this case, we can re-tell the part of the story which the child has told, using the child's own words, and then add a few short sentences describing what the child has done in the pretend play, so as to complete the story. We are in this way modelling the narrative language that the child might have used, and might soon be able to use.

The main aim here is still to show the child that we have paid attention to and respected their pretend play and their story, but now a secondary aim emerges: providing input of slightly more complex language. This is taken even further in the following stage (Expanding) but even at this Modelling stage the focus begins to move gradually towards providing a model not just of stories, but of interaction through language.

The next transcript is from a session with Child B. We see here another example of a child saying "no" to the invitation to tell a story.

In the example above, when Child A says "no", the teacher does not respond but waits quietly, as this is the first time this child has been heard to say "no", and this seems to be the beginning of a sense of agency for this child. However, in the transcript below, where Child B says "no", the teacher responds differently, because this child has said 'no' on several occasions to previous offers to read to him from a picture book, and then shortly afterwards has requested the very same book to be read.

It is difficult to be sure about this, but Child B's "no" has a quite different quality from that of Child A. This example reminds us how much of the work we do with the silent child is thoughtful and informed guesswork; we try to work out what the child needs at any given time and hope we have not got it wrong.

Speaker	Transcript	Strategy
TEACHER	Do you want to tell this story? [The teacher has been reading picture books to this child regularly during their sessions, and this time the teacher presents the child with a set of pictures instead of a book. The pictures, when placed in the correct sequence from left to right, will create a story.]	M: Modelling (invitation to tell a story)
CHILD B	No, I don't want to!	
TEACHER	OK, I'll start. [The teacher wants to show the child that stories need not necessarily be in books with a cover, so she proceeds with this story even though the child has said no. If he had resisted further the best thing to do would have been to pack away the pictures and offer a different book.] Once upon a time, there was a bus.	M: Modelling the story structure
CHILD B	[The child picks up on the story from there and tells the rest of the story with no further prompts from the teacher.] And the bus came, brrr brrr brrr.... [The child then proceeds to tell an entire story on his own, very effectively, with no prompts; at the end of the story he clearly feels happy with his story and looks at the teacher, smiling.]	Child uses the Story Grammar model and begins to tell the story

The following transcript is from a different session with child B in which the teacher again uses a formal story-opening formula to model the story structure. During this session, the child has been playing quietly for quite a while, not talking and not interacting at all.

The teacher waits for some time, hoping for some development in the play, or for an indication that the child acknowledges in some way that she is sitting there with him, but there seems to be no interaction at all on that day.

Once the teacher models the story opening, however, the child not only starts telling his story, but also starts to include the teacher by giving her instructions about joining in the pretend play.

This is progress indeed: the child giving the teacher instructions tells us how much of a sense of agency this child has developed since the start of the programme. The play has become shared play and the story has become a shared story. This giving of instructions to the teacher marks a significant step forward for a child who has only been a passive follower of instructions in the classroom until now.

Speaker	Transcript	Strategy
	[Child B chooses to play with a car. He makes the car drive back and forth, repeatedly. He takes more cars and drives them; this goes on for quite some time; during this time he does not speak at all. He does not look at the teacher, and remains focused on this repetitive play.]	
TEACHER	Once upon a time....	M: Modelling story structure (opening phrase)
CHILD B	The car says... [the child turns to the teacher and says] You play with those cars! [The teacher also picks up a car and make it drive back and forth]	Child starts telling a story Child gives instruction to the teacher to join in the pretend play. Teacher joins in the pretend play.
CHILD B	[The child continues the story] I make a straight [sic] for the cars [using the blocks to make a straight road] I put him... you [addressing the teacher] put your straight line in my cars [He points to the teacher's car and to the road indicating where she should make her car drive]	Child telling a story on his own. Child includes the teacher in the pretend play; interaction through language
CHILD B	I will break the fence now. [The child then tells another entire story independently, without any support, using the same toys but a different plot]	Child telling a story independently

Manyukhina and Wyse (2021) analyse the conditions needed for a person to not only have a sense of agency, but to use this sense of agency as "a socially situated opportunity to act." They suggest that this is a three-fold matter: the first is that the person *believes they are able to act* on the world; the second requirement is they need to live in a world which *will allow them to act*, and the third condition is that the people around them *make opportunities for such action available* [own italics] and ensure that these opportunities are accessible to the child. The transcript above shows that all three of those conditions are present for the child in this stage of the StoryFrames programme.

***

A small detail about the teacher's use of verb tenses in telling these stories: It is not essential to use the past tense when relating a story; some stories can be told equally well in the present tense, (for example, "The car is driving very quickly, and now there is a crash!") However, the use of past tense contributes to the move away from the here-and-now of the immediate play, creating a distance from the concrete, immediate reality; this is an important step in the child's cognitive development.

This point about the use of past or present tense is not critical, as our main aims are to continue to develop the child's sense of confidence in social interaction, and to promote the use of language by the child within this interaction. Issues such as correct grammar and morphology are not part of this programme.

***

Summary of the Modelling stage

In this stage we have started to explicitly model for the child how stories are told in language; we present to the child both the concept of story (that a person can invite a story, or tell a story, or listen to a story) and also Story Grammar (that stories usually begin and end with some typical phrases, and contain characters, and settings, and events which occur in sequential order).

Because the child is by now feeling relaxed in the social situation of teacher and child interacting in the secluded space, and because the child has by now experienced both the use of their own voice and the interaction with the teacher's voice, this stage usually emerges quite smoothly from the previous stages. If there is any reversion to silence on the part of the child, we can always feel free to use the strategies of earlier stages for a while and build back towards the Modelling stage slowly.

***

CHAPTER 12

E is for Expanding

The Expanding stage is the final stage of the programme.

The word 'expanding' describes the extent to which the child has 'expanded' their competence in two vital respects: Not only have they expanded their willingness to interact with others, but they have also expanded their knowledge of the new language.

This is the stage in which we witness the child "coming to voice" (Bakhtin 1981), the stage in which the child has developed a more active sense of agency, can interact freely with both teachers and with other children, and can express their identity as an active inhabitant of the classroom and playground space.

The use of the word "Expanding" here carries several meanings in addition to the concept described above.

- The duration of time spent on this stage can, if resources are available, be 'expanded' well beyond what might be seen as a successful outcome of the programme, when the child is interacting socially and communicatively with other children. The reason for doing this is that children at this age are still developing their social and interactional skills; as children develop, the ways in which social interaction takes place change too. The previously isolated child might benefit from a little more time and support in order to enable them to move along this trajectory together with the other children in their class.
- Another reason for continuing the programme once the aims have been achieved is that once a good rapport has been built up between the teacher and the child in the programme, it may be the case that the child feels that this particular teacher is the person with whom they most want to communicate. The child might continue to feel that the special secluded setting, and the adult to whom they have become attached, are still an important part of their time at school. This did seem to be the case for Child B who, even towards the end of the programme, was more communicative in the sessions than in the classroom. He regularly asked whether he might come back to the "cave" to play with the teacher, even after the programme had ended. The option to expand the programme by continuing to develop ever more co-constructed stories can only benefit the child and help them to develop their language skills even further.
- A further sense in which this idea of 'expanding' presents itself is in the variety of strategies that can be used at this stage of the programme. There are several ways in which teachers can expand on this programme. Teachers should now feel free to add their own ideas and activities at this stage. They will have come to know the child well, and will find many appropriate activities and different ways to use narrative, which can all benefit the child.

- The final achievement of Expanding is when the child is able to take their new-found skills out of the safe space of the StoryFrames sessions, and to do in the classroom and the playground what they have started to do in the sessions with the teacher: to interact freely with others, to make their wishes and thoughts known, and to be active and verbal members of their classroom community.

Co-constructing the stories

It is during this Expanding stage that the teacher and child begin to *co-construct* the story. This is not to say that the teacher should ever overrule the child's choice of topic or ideas in the story; however the teacher can now feel free to make suggestions and to ask a few more questions, while always being careful not to be intrusive, and not to give the child the feeling that the teacher is suggesting that the story needs to be improved. The aim is to achieve a shared creative experience, where each participant has a voice, but where the initial choices and the final decisions remain those of the child.

Communication is a complex matter, and in situations such as these teachers can only use their sensitivity to guide them when to take a next step and when it might seem stressful or intrusive to the child. The response of the child to each step, if carefully monitored, gives us clues as to whether our expansion is the right thing at the right time, or whether we need to take a step back.

What emerges from this Expanding stage, therefore, is perhaps the most significant mark of the success of the programme: the narrative is still rooted in the child's own ideas, but the teacher and child begin to contribute more equally to the progress of the story and to participate in a kind of conversation, and in a shared creative endeavour.

Both participants are now actively involved in building the story: both are adding ideas and suggesting changes. The child, at this stage, becomes a truly assertive communication partner, which is our wished-for outcome for the previously silent child.

Here are some of the strategies we can use to co-construct a story with the child:

- Think about what might be **the next event in the story**. We can use simple lead-in phrases ("And then...") or ask a pondering type of question ("I wonder what they will do next...") The pondering attitude is much less intrusive and controlling than a direct question.
- Introduce **the vocabulary of feelings**. For example, the teacher might say, "I wonder what the turtle is feeling..." or make a questioning, tentative suggestion ("Maybe that turtle is sad...")
- Use a 'pondering' suggestion to **add a new idea or character** to the child's story. One could, for example, pick a toy from the set which has not been used in the child's story, and say something like "I wonder if this dog wants to be in the story" or "I wonder if this car can also drive on the road..." The child is of course free to agree or not to agree to the suggestion.
- Expand the story by **asking for more information about any character or event** in the story. We have discussed in the previous chapters the use of only closed (yes-no)

questions; we can now feel free to expand our use of questions and ask 'why' and 'how' and even 'why not' questions, always being careful not to be too intrusive and not to ask too many questions.

Inviting the child to tell their story again, at a time separate from the pretend play

In this strategy, we might remind a child of a story they had told in a previous session and ask them to tell the story again, because we liked that story, or perhaps so that we can write it down this time.

This strategy makes a more explicit demand of the child, something we have avoided doing until now. It is, in a way, asking the child to perform for the teacher. The shy or quiet child may automatically 'shut down' when such demands are placed on them. However, by this stage in the programme, the child is usually familiar with the situation and can take this in their stride.

This step is important, as it sets down, for the first time, a kind of agenda for the session: the child is free to play as usual, but we have re-framed the experience within a genre of performance, to be shared with another person, as opposed to a private experience.

In addition, the re-telling of a story at a later date contributes to the child's sense of the stability and predictability of experience over time: the child is not just living the immediate experience of what they are playing with, but is looking back, remembering, and repeating something which was important for them. We are here making an assumption relating to the child's recent life experience: that re-locating from a different country and a different language might have been a terrifying experience, in which nothing was predictable or consistent. The experience of re-telling a story can hint at the possibility that memories can also be happy ones, or that the trajectory of a story can be changed and a preferred story can be created (Morgan 2000; Marston et al, 2016).

Writing down the story for the child

Once the child has started telling their story using spoken language, we can move to another strategy: the option for the teacher to write down the child's story. In this way we move further towards meta-cognition and abstraction: we started with physical pretend play, we then moved to spoken language, and now we move from spoken to written language.

The act of writing the story down makes it permanent; the pretend play has thus been transformed into something which becomes for the child a visible proof of their agency.

In some cases, the child does not easily enter the stage of telling their story in words if it is at a time separated from the play (for example, in the next session). They may not remember the story at all. If this happens, the teacher can write the child's stories directly after they have been told, in the same session, and read them to the child in the next session.

The reading aloud from printed picture books (see Chapter Five) becomes even more important at this stage, as we are providing additional models for the child of the way a story might be told, retold, and recorded.

Making a paper book with the child's story

The subsequent creation of a picture book which contains the child's own story serves to make concrete their achievement: they can carry it around with them, take it home, and show other people what they have created. A simple stapled paper book is easy to make (see below * for some links on how to do this) and serves as tangible evidence for the child that their story was something real, and remains so long after the play has ended, even after the child has left the safe space and returned to the classroom. The hand-made book can, in this way, become a "transitional object" for the child (Winnicott 1957).

Ideally, the child will be able to retell their story, using the book as a prompt, to people other than the teacher who is running the programme. The book can then serve as a bridge to carry the child away from the secluded safe space, and generalise their new skills in interacting with and speaking to others.

Many children in the programme have shown great joy and pride in having their own book, with their own story. Some have enjoyed 'reading' the book to their family, or even to another teacher, and this repeated re-telling of their story provides for them additional experience of "language output" (Swain 2001).

Of course there are some obvious difficulties in making a book on the spot: it takes time, and we do not want the child to get bored, or to be a passive observer while the teacher makes the book. It is also difficult to write legibly when we are trying to finish the book quickly, before the session ends. But by making a book while the child is watching, and involving the child where possible, we are not only showing the child an interesting and creative process, but also introducing the child to mark-making.

There are various ways to involve the child in the actual process of making the book so that they are not passive observers of the process: The child can choose the colour and size of paper for the inner pages; we can offer a range of different types and colours of card for the cover, pre-cut to different sizes and shapes. The child can safely help to use the stapler or hole-punch while we do the actual stapling, by pushing down on top of our hand.

An additional benefit is for the child to see how we actually write. By saying each word aloud, or sounding out the separate letters while we write, we are introducing the child to writing and spelling. The intention is of course not, at this stage, to teach the child to write, but to keep the child involved and interested while the book is being made.

If we are concerned about the legibility and aesthetic qualities of a quickly-made handwritten book there is another option: to hand-write the text and create the book during the session, with the participation of the child, but to later type and print the text, add a cover and present the child with an additional printed version of the same story. This is something to consider: are we reducing the value of the original book by creating a copy? Perhaps we might suggest that the printed copy can be kept by the child at home, and the hand-written copy be carried around at school? These are decisions which can be made at the time.

The teacher can also ask the child if they want to add a dedication and to choose a title for the book: For example, "This book is for Daddy" or "This is my story" or "The scary monster".

In this way we are including the child in every aspect of their book, and replicating the actual process of book-writing.

It is also helpful and fun to include simple illustrations on each page, although for those of us who struggle to draw, this is a challenge. One way around it is this: when you notice, over one or two sessions, what the child's story will be about; you can prepare ahead of time a few small printed pictures, downloaded from any online source, and while making the book, glue them onto the page. Alternatively, the child can be invited to illustrate their own book.

Another way to include illustrations is to practice drawing stick figures which are relatively easy to copy. If you do an online search for "How to draw cartoon stick figures" you will find many easy-to-copy drawings. Here is an example: https://www.youtube.com/watch?v=wXwX0NV7SEg

An enjoyable option is to make miniature books. (See Appendix V for some information about miniature books made by the writer Charlotte Bronte and her siblings.) Miniature books conceptually match the miniature world of the tiny toys, and I have found that they are often objects of fascination to the child. A miniature book obviously leaves little space for the writing of the words of the story, but can include simple stick-figure illustrations of the basic elements of the story. The child's memory of their pretend play will fill in any gaps.

* Here are some links for quick, simple and low-cost ways to make a book with paper and card. You will find many other examples online.

https://youtu.be/MjZmber59_s
https://youtu.be/ofQwGKZsvuw
https://youtu.be/eBs9OaFJ6rc

***

The social use of language

In this Expanding stage of the programme, once the child has gone beyond simple sentences describing what the toy characters are doing, and can now participate in a conversation, there is a different kind of communication skill which becomes relevant. This is called the 'social use of language'.

The social use of language refers to how the speaker makes use of language in order to socialise with other people. This is sometimes called "functional language" as the language used is serving a social function. An example of the social use of language would be greeting: saying hello and goodbye appropriately. Another aspect of social language use is saying no, or refusing, or disagreeing. The ability to say 'no' to something unwanted, to refuse to comply, or to reject an unwelcome suggestion from another person, is a critically important aspect of self-advocacy and safety, and one which some children find very difficult.

Other social uses of language are drawing the attention of someone to something interesting; describing things; explaining things; or giving information. The ability to use language socially is specific to each culture, and this knowledge goes beyond simply knowing how to speak a language.

The act of requesting (asking for a toy, or asking to join in the game of another child) is also a social use of language. This requires the child to have not only sufficient language; there is also a need for the child to know the socially accepted ways of joining a game in the new culture, and also to have a large measure of confidence to make such a request, with the knowledge that the answer may be a 'yes' or a 'no'.

Learning how to socially negotiate joining in the games of other children is a very difficult and subtle process; different cultures have different ways of joining in. The silent child might well take a while to learn this skill, even once their language has reached a desired level. For this reason it might be helpful for the teacher running the StoryFrames programme to enlist the class teacher's help in making sure that the once-silent child does indeed begin to join in the games of the other children, and perhaps assist if necessary. In such situations, a few additional StoryFrames sessions can be useful if the teacher expands the stories to include some examples of how a child might ask to join in a game.

The use of appropriate loudness of voice is another social use of language which differs among cultures. Child A, at the start of the programme, used only a very quiet voice. She would fall silent and sit motionless (the 'freeze' defence mechanism) if anyone walked past the "cave" where the sessions were being held. For this child it seemed that using a quiet voice was a way to avoid being noticed, and to avoid the perhaps intrusive attentions of other people. In the early sessions she sometimes used no voice at all, using instead gesture and nods to respond to questions.

Over time she began to use a louder and more confident voice during the sessions, and later still she was also able to use her voice when other people were in the vicinity. However it took her time to begin using an audible voice when she returned to the classroom after each session. She did later achieve this, and by the end of the programme she was also able to adjust the loudness of her voice according to the social situation, using an appropriately quieter voice when in the classroom, and a louder voice when playing outside in the playground.

Turn-taking

An important aspect of the social use of language is 'turn-taking'. This refers to the back-and-forth nature of everyday conversation, where participants often take turns: one speaks while the other listens; then the listener responds, and it is the turn of the initial speaker to listen. Both parties in this way build on each other's contributions in a turn-taking conversation (Alexander 2003).

As seen in the transcripts, in the initial sessions of the programme the children speak very little, and when they do speak, there is very little conversation. The children in the early stages usually talk about their pretend play, and are perhaps talking more to themselves than to the teacher. Turn-taking is an aspect of recognition that there is another person in my space, with whom I need to share the interaction.

Slowly, as the teacher progresses through the stages of Repeating, Adding, Modelling and Expanding, the speaking becomes more conversational, with both parties taking part, each of them making "consecutive contributions" (Engel 1995 p 129). The child may say something, the teacher may respond or ask a question, and the child then responds to the teacher's response.

It is this kind of turn-taking which is seen in the joint construction of meaning which Wells (1985) describes as so crucial in further language development. In the Expanding stage, both the child and the adult are taking equal responsibility for the storytelling.

The next transcript is an example of Child B showing the lack of turn-taking in his early stages of the programme. While his language is now approaching an appropriate age level in terms of grammar and sentence length, the entire story is told without looking at the teacher at all, and without checking if the teacher is listening, or interested, or even present. At this stage in the programme, the child does not yet engage in any reciprocal alternation of turns. He talks at length, and will talk over the teacher's voice if the teacher does speak.

Happily, at the end of this session, the child does start to include the teacher in the story, and this is the first sign of his ability to use the social skill of turn-taking.

Speaker	Transcript	Strategy
	[The teacher reads to Child B from two different picture books, one about cars and the other about trucks. During this time, the child looks at the books but does not look at the teacher at all.]	
CHILD B	[The child picks up two miniature cars] Somebody crash into the orange car! And they crash!	
CHILD B	[Takes a post-it note and draws some lines. The child makes no eye contact at all with the teacher but picks up the drawing] I making a road on my paper	
CHILD B	And there... some police came off his line [sic]	
CHILD B	[He takes the toy airplane from the toy box] Three police came with the airplane, and the other one came out of the hospital to see.	
CHILD B	Get out!! Get out!! [gesturing as if to people in the cars, who must get out to be safe]	
CHILD B	The doctors came out of their car And they wait for somebody to come	
CHILD B	Look! I make the airplane stay on that car... [Child B now looks at the teacher, points to the plane and checks if she has noticed what he is referring to] They drived [sic] away.	Child uses gaze shift and "look!" to share joint attention with the teacher. He is interacting with her for the first time in this session.

In order to help such a child develop turn-taking skills, the teacher can make extensive use of the earlier strategies of Repeating and Adding in order to indicate that there is another person in this space, someone who is listening, and someone with whom the child can share their ideas.

A very different sequence of turns is seen in the following transcript, where, if we look at the "Speaker" column, we can see the regular alternation of speakers. In this example, the sequence is very regular: child/ teacher /child /teacher.

Speaker	Transcript	Strategy
CHILD A	He scared, he want this [The child picks up the frog and the blanket]	
TEACHER	He's scared.	R: Repeating
CHILD A	And he have blanket, put it on here [The child covers the frog with the blanket]	
TEACHER	Put it here Cover him up	R: Repeating A: Adding words
CHILD A	They scared, there's a monster coming!	
TEACHER	They're hiding from a monster.	A: Adding words

In the transcript above, the child and the teacher are participating in a very regular and equal allocation of turns. This is deliberately organised by the teacher in order to introduce the skill of turn-taking, through the techniques of Repetition and of Adding to the child's words.

The reason for this deliberate engineering of regular alternative turns is that the silent child has little or no experience of turn-taking in the new language being learned, due to their total lack of participation in any kind of conversation at school. The artificial manipulation of turn-taking serves as a model for the child in how conversations can be managed.

However this artificial model of turn-taking cannot be said to be true dialogic turn-taking in Alexander's sense (2004) or true joint meaning-making in Wells' sense (1985). In real life, this is not how turn-taking actually proceeds. Two people communicating effectively with each other will indeed take turns, but the turns are usually adjusted according to whether the speaker feels that the listener has understood, or whether the speaker needs to explain something further.

For example, the listener may need more information, which might lead the speaker to take a very long turn, without a break, while the speaker takes on a listening-only role. If a listener wants to indicate that they have now understood, or are bored with the conversation, or if the listener strongly disagrees which what was said, they may interrupt the other person's turn.

It is surprising to learn that socially competent speakers, having a calm and polite conversation, also often overlap each other's turn. In recordings of any two adult speakers in a conversation, we see that the turns often overlap: the listener begins their turn before the speaker has finished a turn, because the listener has understood the gist of what is being said and is ready to reply. Schegloff (2000) provides a more detailed analysis of this.

The mere presence of turn-taking is not enough, therefore, to satisfy; it is the quality of the turn-taking which matters. It needs to be something which both of the participants in a conversation actively do: both talking and both listening, in turn, in an attempt to fully understand each other, while at the same time ensuring that their ideas are fully heard.

The next transcript shows Child B moving towards the kind of turn-taking which we see in more accomplished social conversations: we start to see here the quality of a dialogue. Both parties take turns, in a relatively orderly fashion, and both parties listen to and respond to each other, but no single person dominates the conversation.

Speaker	Transcript	Strategy
CHILD B	[The child is playing with toy cars and helicopters, telling the teacher what he has got at home] I don't got a helicopter.	
TEACHER	You haven't got a helicopter. Have you got a plane?	R: Repeating E: Expanding
CHILD B	I don't got a plane. Because me and my daddy got a big bike, so don't go there. [sic]	
TEACHER	Does the big bike go fast?	E: Expanding
CHILD B	No no, cause we went up the hill and we went straight down [some unintelligible talk]	Turn-taking and social use of language: answering the question asked by the teacher

The next transcript is another example of the now accomplished dialogic turn-taking during the Expanding stage of the programme with Child B:

Speaker	Transcript	Strategy
TEACHER	[The teacher points to a picture in a picture book] Look, what's happening here? Let's have a look	
CHILD B	And they- then they have to give theirself [sic] petrol for the car [The child quickly turns 2 pages]	
TEACHER	I want to go in that green car and you go in that red car	E: Expanding
CHILD B	OK	Social interaction: agreeing
CHILD B	I'm going to- oh oh!!! Look! They crashed into the car!	Social use of language: Child points out something to the teacher
TEACHER	Oh my goodness! [Child picks up the police car and starts driving] Who is coming?	F: Feelings E: Expanding
CHILD B	The police, I want to be the policeman, you have to crash into the r..... you crash into the ...[pause] ...the orange car	Social use of language: giving instructions
TEACHER	I'll crash into the orange car and you be the policeman. What did he say to these people?	R: Repeating E: Expanding (open question)
CHILD B	You have to move- you have to move your car, you have to draw some, somefink here to there	Child invites the adult to play and to draw
TEACHER	What should we draw?	E: Expanding (open question)
CHILD B	Draw the policeman. [The teacher draws a picture of a policeman; the child puts it next to the police car] On my TV I saw somebody sitting in – I saw somebody sitting in the back!	The Child shares a real event with a listener: social use of language
TEACHER	Why did he sit in the back?	E: Expanding (open question)
CHILD B	Because they was naughty, crash into the... the... the... [long silent pause]	
TEACHER	Let's count the cars.	E: Expanding
CHILD B	[Child counts very competently to 12]	

***

To summarise, in this chapter we have looked at a range of strategies which can be used to expand the narratives of the children we are working with, once they have reached the stage where they are confident in spoken interaction.

By this stage the children usually appear to have developed a sense of their own agency, and in addition their spoken language has often developed considerably in terms of vocabulary and grammar. They are also now starting to use language socially; the talk in the sessions has expanded to become a socially interactive dialogue.

We can now expect the child to begin taking their new-found skills out of the secluded space and into the classroom. We can expect to see them interacting with other children and with the teacher to a much greater extent than prior to the programme. This is an important next step and the assistance of the child's class teacher may be needed to ensure that this does take place. As described above, a teacher may use a 'buddy system' and enlist the help of a socially empathetic child to help with this integration into the classroom.

During the process of the StoryFrames programme, communication between the child's class teacher and the person running the programme is crucial, in order to enable the child to seamlessly transition from the sessions in the secluded space, to the more unstructured and unprotected space of the classroom. It is important not to assume that the child will automatically transfer their new skills to the classroom and the playground. The class teacher should be informed of the main principles of the StoryFrames programme, and kept up to date with the child's progress, so that they can then support the child in taking their next steps in social integration.

The following chapter presents some examples of transcripts which showcase the achievements of these two children during the six weeks in which they attended StoryFrames sessions.

***

CHAPTER 13

A showcase of achievement

The following transcripts show the emergence of the two children in the original research programme from their Silent Period, as they reached the final sessions of the StoryFrames programme.

Of course, the ultimate challenge would be whether they were subsequently able to use their new-found confidence and language skills in the classroom and in the playground. We will see, from the teacher checklists completed a few months after the programme had ended, that this was indeed the case.

The following transcript shows Child A's emerging language early in the Expanding stage of the programme. There are many pauses, while she tries to find the words and sentence structures she needs to tell her story. During these pauses, the teacher does not attempt to help or to advise, but rather allows the child to take her own time. This accepting attitude, of patient listening, provides for the child the kind of atmosphere where she is under no pressure to talk. In spite of the hesitant language, we see that the child is fully engaged in expressing her ideas about the experience of the characters in her story. If we can look past the many pauses and her difficulty with the language, we can see a fully-formed story emerging, in which she expresses the experience of fictional characters and also her own life experience of birthdays and family beliefs.

Speaker	Transcript	Strategy
CHILD A	[She picks up a toy gecko] It his birthday, he … [pause] he is now nine. [She covers the table with a tissue, takes a flower, breaks it into little pieces and puts it on the 'table'; she joins two tissues together with a sticker to make a bigger tablecloth] This … [pause] some sweeties. [She picks up another toy, a dog] Your birthday is not now.	
TEACHER	[Waits a while, then asks] Not now? When is it?	E: Expanding (open question)
CHILD A	[Long pause] Tomorrow. You sleep and you … [long pause] Then … [long pause] … you sleep…[long pause] You …[pause]… you need to sleep this morning, then the angels come … [pause] then the angels will wake you up and say "It [sic] your birthday today!"	

***

The next transcript is from a session in the Expanding stage of the programme with Child B. We see in this example how the child and the teacher are jointly constructing the story, although in keeping with the principles of this programme the teacher is still following the child's lead in the choice of toys and topic. The teacher now begins to expand the story beyond what the child has shown or said, and we see how the child interacts, agreeing or disagreeing with the teacher, in a confident voice, making his wishes known through his own sense of agency, and his now competent use of language and the narrative form.

Speaker	Transcript	Strategy
CHILD B	[Picks up a picture book which had been read the week before, about a man who flies a plane] I don't want to read it again. [Begins to play with cars and helicopter, and a dinosaur]	
TEACHER	[The teacher puts the book away. She watches what the child is doing with the toys, and then describes what the child is doing] One day, there was a helicopter and a car, and they went flying in the sky. The dinosaur said, "Can I catch you?" And he tried to jump but he couldn't catch them because they were flying in the sky.	M: Modelling narrative structure
CHILD B	[Child gives a dinosaur to the teacher] You have that one!	Child chooses to co-construct the story
TEACHER	And then the dinosaur said to the car, "Can I drive on your back?"	E: Expanding
CHILD B	[The child drives the car, crashes into the dinosaur and throws it to the side.] Wooo Wooo Woooo!!!	
TEACHER	Wooo! So he went up in the sky again. The end.	R: Repeating E: Expanding M: Modelling story structure (story ending)
CHILD B	No! The police!! [He picks up the police car and crashes into the two dinosaurs] I want to take this and you can have the car and I have...... [pause] you have that car and I have..... [He divides the cars so that we each have some cars]	Agency: The child resists ending the story in the way the teacher suggested. The child co-constructs the story

In the above transcript we have clear evidence of the child's growing belief in his own ability to "negotiate meaning" (Lave and Wenger 1991). This ability to negotiate meaning indicates that the child has developed a sense of his own agency, and that he knows that his voice and wishes deserve to be and will be heard and respected. It is this sense of agency, emerging by the end of the programme, which is the indication of the success of the programme.

***

An example of Child B's now-developed use of turn-taking can be seen in the following excerpt, in which he asks the adult a question and then looks at the adult and waits for the answer. He then rejects her suggestion to tell a different story but gives her a reason for his rejection ("when I finished playing").

The turns are now being taken with an understanding of what the other person in the conversation might need in order to keep the communication flowing smoothly.

In this same transcript, once the child is satisfied that he has told his story, he explicitly tells the teacher, "I finished!" This is a clear indication that this child has now integrated the story structure into his cognitive awareness, by being able to use aspects of Story Grammar: in this case, a formal ending. He then confidently uses the imperative form "Look!" to include the teacher in the story. Here we see his willingness to spontaneously interact with another person; he is able to use the new language, and to use it with confidence and with agency. His "Look!" is a verbal invitation to another person to share joint attention, not only to what he has done, but to the pleasure and pride he feels in what he has done. The triumph on his face when saying this indicates that he now has the awareness of a story as something outside of the immediacy of the pretend play, and can take pleasure from something he has created.

He next tells the teacher that he is now ready to hear a new story. This is an example of the social use of language: making a request for something from a teacher. This child, when in his silent period, requested nothing, but rather waited passively for decisions to be made for him. He now not only allows the teacher to 'enter' the story and to add ideas and events to the story, but actively invites this.

In this sense, the child's once solitary play has now 'Expanded' to become a truly interactive socially communicative and verbal activity, shared between the two participants. We see in this transcript evidence of the hoped-for outcome of the StoryFrames programme: confident communication, the sharing of ideas and feelings, evidence of a sense of agency, and using the language of the classroom to do all of this.

These outcomes are the very opposite of what we understand as "the Silent Period".

Speaker	Transcript	Strategy
CHILD B	[The child chooses a car] Beep beep beep ... [The child now sees the toy ducks on the shelf; the teacher had been keeping those aside to use as props for another story] Why do you got the ducks? [The child looks at the teacher when asking the question]	Child actively asks for information. Eye gaze shifts to the teacher when asking.
TEACHER	It's for a duck story. Shall I tell you the story?	E: Expanding (closed question)
CHILD B	Not now, after, when I finished playing.	Child's sense of agency: saying no, and explaining why
TEACHER	OK, you tell me when you're ready.	E: Expanding Explicitly recognising the child's agency
CHILD B	.... And some people is opening the door and I can't get in. I finished! Look! [He looks at teacher, then points to the red bus] The red bus is the same like the fire engine! [The child shares an observation with the teacher]	Child indicates that his story has ended by using an appropriate Story Grammar sentence. Uses "Look" and pointing as invitation to share joint attention with the teacher Social use of language: sharing ideas; sharing what he has observed and found interesting.
TEACHER	Yes, it's red, It's the same colour.	R: Repeating E: Expanding
CHILD B	And the tree is green. And I ready for the duck story!	Social use of language: continuing to talk on a topic of common interest Social use of language: making a request

***

The following transcript is from a session with Child A, during the Expanding stage of the programme, showing the child actually suggesting to the teacher a way to expand her story. The expansion here involves the child co-constructing the story by inviting the teacher to give a name to one of the toys, and then saying that she, the child, will write her own name. We see here the dual aims of the programme being achieved: the child is confidently initiating social interaction, and is using language to do so.

Speaker	Transcript	Strategy
TEACHER	[Teacher reads a picture book to the child.]	
CHILD A	[Child A listens intently but silently. Then she starts playing with the toy furniture and characters, and uses the fabric to make a tent] Turtle got in the bed, cover turtle with a blanket! [The toy table, which she is pretending is a bed, falls over] It's breaking! Oh no!	
TEACHER	It's breaking! Turtle fell out!	R: Repeating A: Adding words
CHILD A	Yeah!	
TEACHER	Can we fix it?	E: Expanding (closed question)
CHILD A	So he slept on a mattress.	
TEACHER	He can sleep on a mattress.	R: Repeating
CHILD A	So... so... he...you can give turtle a name, and I write my name. [She hands the teacher the post-it notes and the pencil to write down the name of the turtle, and then she writes her own name beneath the turtle's name]	Social use of language The child co-constructs the story with the teacher.
TEACHER	Turtle's name is Goomy. And he can sleep on the mattress.	E: Expanding
CHILD A	Oh, oh! The mattress is breaking too!! [She shakes the mattress]	
TEACHER	Oh dear! Has he got somewhere else to sleep?	F: Feelings E: Expanding
CHILD A	Nothing!! [Meaning that he has nowhere to sleep]	

***

The next example, also from Child A, takes place during the Expanding stage, in which the teacher takes a more directive stance, making suggestions and even asking some open questions ("why").

At this stage in the programme this child is speaking confidently, using a greater variety of vocabulary and longer sentences, with fewer pauses. She is spontaneously telling the teacher about various events that had happened at home, with her family. This example shows that once the child emerges from the silence, and has regained their sense of agency, the conversations in the sessions become much more free and spontaneous, both for the teacher and for the child. The use of the set of tiny toys becomes less important, and the incidence of free conversation, of dialogue, becomes more frequent.

Note also the advanced level of English language this child is now using, compared to the very short sentences and limited vocabulary she had been using only six weeks prior to this session.

Speaker	Transcript	Strategy
CHILD A	[Takes out of the toy box the miniature bunk bed.] We did go on holiday in Norfolk and I did sleep in a bunk bed.	
TEACHER	A bunk bed? Like this one?	Closed question
CHILD A	And I did bump my head, and I couldn't stand!	
TEACHER	You couldn't stand? Oh my goodness!	R: Repeating F: Feelings
CHILD A	And my sister too.	
TEACHER	Did she sleep in the bunk bed too?	E: Expanding (closed question; the child could have answered with yes/no; However she chooses to give a much more complete answer)
CHILD A	No, she did sleep with my mommy and daddy. And then we need to close the door and I don't like door closed.	Social use of language: sharing information
TEACHER	Don't you? Why not?	E: Expanding (closed question) E: Expanding (open question "why")
CHILD A	Why it's too dark, I wanna see my Sheepy. [Sheepy is her security blanket which she has been bringing to the sessions over the last few weeks]	Sharing information
TEACHER	And did you close the door?	E: Expanding (Closed question)
CHILD A	No!	

***

The next transcript, from child B, recorded as the programme was ending, took place in the classroom and not in the "cave". It is an example of the expansion of both language and interaction skills achieved by this previously silent child. He was now able not only to talk to and play with other children, but also to be bolder in his interactions: to take initiative and give instructions to other children as to what to do or say.

We see here that the Expanding strategy has now been fully realised: the child has taken his new-found agency out of the "cave" and into the classroom; he is using his agency and his communication skills not only with the teacher who runs the programme but with other children and in the presence of his class teacher. This is the true meaning of "Expanding": the generalisation, or expansion, of the child's communicative interaction skills from the safe secluded space of the programme sessions, into the daily life of the classroom or the playground.

Speaker	Transcript
	[The therapist enters the classroom to say hello to the class teacher. Child B is sitting next to another child, both on the teacher's chair, and they are pretending to be the teacher. They are seated facing two other children who are playing the role of students. We see here Child B taking charge, being assertive and speaking fluently.]
CHILD B	[Talking to the other child who is also playing teacher] They all standing up! [The other child tells the 'students' to sit down]
CHILD B	[Giving instructions to the other children, to be polite and to stand up when the 'teacher' is talking to them] Get up. Max was talking. Max talking now!
CHILD B	[The other child who is taking a teacher role starts reading from a picture book but skips a page; Child B notices this immediately and comments on it.] No! We forgot that page- we didn't do fluffy hats! Go back!

***

CHAPTER 14

A window onto an inner world

In looking back at some of the transcripts from the StoryFrames programme, we see that there are some themes which dominate the stories told by the two children, Child A and Child B. These stories give us a glimpse into their inner world.

Although it has been stressed that the StoryFrames programme is very different from play therapy, and that the aim of the programme is *not* to look too closely at the themes appearing in the pretend play and stories told by the children, but rather to encourage them to tell any story they wish to, it does seem in some way relevant to look at some of the themes which emerged repeatedly in the stories of these two silent children. We must, at the very least, acknowledge that these children are telling us something.

There is a risk of being so pleased that the child is emerging from their silence that we focus more on their language and friendships, and forget to listen to what they have been saying.

Colette Granger writes extensively about these issues for silent children (2004). She studies the narratives told by now-adult second language learners who have chosen to express their experiences of being new to a country and to a language, through their diaries or autobiographic writing. Their writing can show us something about what a child in the Silent Period might be experiencing.

Granger's focus is not so much on the difficulties involved in the acquisition of the new language, but on the losses which the person experiences in the move to a new place, where their own language is not spoken or understood. Granger writes that "... the traumatic event that narrative holds and later interprets is the loss of the self that dwelled in the first language..." (Granger 2004).

In looking at the dominant themes in the narratives of these two children, we see themes of car crashes, fires, loss, and death. There are stories of being too small and of having nowhere to sleep. Most of Child A's stories seem to be fictional, with a few stories which she explicitly says are about events which had happened in her own family. Towards the end of the programme she was relating more personal and family narratives. Child B on the other hand frequently told personal narratives, although some of his narratives contained both personal and seemingly fictitious events within the same story.

Perhaps these different types of stories (narratives of personal or autobiographical experience, and narratives which are fictional) are not that different from one another. The view taken here is that both types of narrative show how the child is "making sense of the world" (Engel 1995 p 28). There is an overriding feeling that these children are thinking hypothetically through their stories: they are using "possibility thinking" such as "what if" and "what can I do with this?" (Jeffrey and Craft 2004).

This repetition of pretend play and of stories is to be expected within the StoryFrames programme. Whitehead suggests that "repeating and re-assembling the events of a story is a significant way of thinking about things and sorting them out" (Whitehead 2002). Through stories, children make sense of their world. If they need to re-visit a story because they do not feel they have resolved whatever they are pondering, that is their choice.

Paley (1981) talks about the themes which emerge from children's stories: "...The themes are vast and wondrous. Images of good and evil, birth and death, parent and child, move in and out of the real and the pretend. There is no small talk." Similarly, Gotschall (2013) says that children's pretend play and stories are often about "only one thing: trouble". Through their narrative play we can get a hint of their thoughts about a world of confusion, disorder, and fear.

Most of the stories are emotionally touching. The following excerpt gives us an example of how much feeling we are privileged to be witness to in this kind of close interaction with a child. The teacher reads a picture book to Child B about a young baby, and this might have brought up some feelings for Child B about being small and dependent. His rather strong reaction is surely some expression of the discomfort this story brings up in him.

Speaker	Transcript
	[Picture book: The book uses the repeated phrase "when I was young" and talks about how the child no longer does babyish things like crying, lying in bed, drinking from a bottle etc]
CHILD B	[The child listens to the whole story, saying nothing. Then he takes the book out of the teacher's hands, closes it firmly and puts it in the teacher's bag. He closes the bag and checks to make sure it is closed.] Don't never [sic] bring that book no more!
TEACHER	I won't bring that one any more. [The teacher then reads to him from a non-fiction book about the foods we like to eat, hoping to provide something emotionally neutral after the previous upsetting book; he seems to relax now and to enjoy listening to the second book.]

A predominant theme in the stories of both children is death. Here is Child A:

Speaker	Transcript	
CHILD A	[Playing with a plastic fish] I want to eat, I'm hungry. I wa... [pause] I'm hungry. I want some... [pause] to eat, I wanna EAT YOU UP! [She puts the fish on the teacher's arm and pretends to eat her arm, fingers, and hand].	
TEACHER	Oh my goodness! And then...	F: Feelings A: Adding words
CHILD A	Then he was died. This- this fish was died. And then he was didn't die.	
TEACHER	And then what happened?	E: Expanding (open question)
CHILD A	And he didn't die; This is the end of the story.	Story Grammar ending

The theme of disorder or violence appears in nearly every one of Child B's stories. Nicolopoulou (1997) in her analysis of boys' stories talks of "a fascination for disorder".

Speaker	Transcript	
CHILD B	[Playing with two cars] I'm going to- oh oh!!! Look! They crashed into the car [Child B picks up the police car and drives it towards the crashed car]	Child inviting joint attention: "look!"
TEACHER	Who is coming?	E: Expanding (open question)
CHILD B	The police, I want to be the police man, you have to crash into the car… [pause] you crash into the –[pause] the orange car	Co-constructing a story
TEACHER	I'll crash into the orange car and you be the policeman……	Co-constructing a story

Issues of power and mastery are another recurring theme. An analysis by Whitehead of "what children do" with their stories suggests that their symbolic representations "play a vital role in their efforts to make sense of the world and to find their place in it." (Whitehead 2002). The next transcript is an example of the how the theme of power emerges in Child B's stories:

Speaker	Transcript	Strategy
	[The child asks the teacher to draw a picture of a shark on a post-it note. He is playing with some of the miniature animals.]	
CHILD B	Then the shark go back in the field	
TEACHER	He went back in the field. Bye bye shark! [The teacher crosses out the shark]	R: Repeating E: Expanding
CHILD B	And daddy cow came and eat the shark up and the shark is all in his tummy now.	

The following story, told by Child A, hints perhaps at her feeling the lack of power and agency in her everyday life at school. Her story is about being small, about wanting to be bigger (and thus perhaps more powerful) but the character in this story does not succeed, and remains, in spite of all her efforts, small.

Speaker	Transcript	Strategy
CHILD A	[Picks up a small dinosaur] Can we the bigger? [sic]	
TEACHER	[The teacher indicates non-verbally that she doesn't understand what the child is asking]	
CHILD A	Can we do the animal bigger?	
TEACHER	Make them bigger?	R: Repeating (closed question)
CHILD A	Can we do the animals bigger?	

TEACHER	I don't have any bigger ones. Have you got big ones at home?	E: Expanding (closed question)
CHILD A	[Child A continues to look at the small dinosaur, silently] We can make them bigger.	Child stays on her own topic (indicates a sense of agency.)
TEACHER	How can we? What can we do?	E: Expanding (open question)
CHILD A	I think we can, like, we can, can we say abracadabra make them bigger?	
TEACHER	Oh! We can say abracadabra. You say it.	R: Repeating E: Expanding
CHILD A	Abracadabra! [she waits a moment] He was still tiny!	
CHILD A	I can put him in my crown [on that day the child was wearing a tiara] and I will say abracadabra. [She takes off the tiara, places it on the mat, and puts the dinosaur in the middle of her tiara] ABRACADABRA!! [Very loud voice, unusually for this child] ...And he was still tiny.	
TEACHER	Let's try to put him in your pocket.	E: Expanding
CHILD A	[Puts the dinosaur in her pocket] Abracadabra! He still tiny.	
TEACHER	Oh dear!	F: Feelings
CHILD A	We do it in a magic box. [She puts the dinosaur in the little box] Abracadabra! Oh! Still tiny!	
TEACHER	Dinosaur said, "I want to be big." Maybe... if I eat lots of apples, I can get bigger?	R: Repeating E: Expanding
CHILD A	Look! [Gesturing to the mouth of the dinosaur and then looking at the teacher to see if she has noticed] He can't open his mouth... and he didn't get what - what to eat.	Co-constructing the story: child shares joint attention with and explains to the teacher
TEACHER	[Draws a picture of a glass of water and puts the picture next to the dinosaur] Let's give him something to drink then.	E: Expanding
CHILD A	[Mimes the dinosaur drinking water from a glass] All drinked up! [sic]	
TEACHER	And then?	E: Expanding (open question)
CHILD A	And he didn't get bigger, and the [sic] didn't get bigger.	
TEACHER	Maybe we need to say it very loud?	E: Expanding
CHILD A	[In a very loud voice] ABRACADABRA! [pause] and he was still tiny	
TEACHER	Oh! Poor thing...	F: Feelings
CHILD A	ABRACADBRA! He still tiny! What we gonna do? [Very quiet voice again. The Child throws her hands up in a gesture of despair]	

A more psychoanalytic analysis would probably unearth several more themes from the transcripts. Although this is not the prime focus of the StoryFrames programme, these transcripts do hint at the rich data which is presented when children's stories are recorded verbatim.

Examining these themes provides the unexpected privilege of being offered "glimpses of a complex inner life" (Engel 2005 p 1). Such information would not have been available through purely linguistic or cognitive analyses of narrative skills, using grammatical or Story Grammar frameworks. The possible symbolic meaning of these themes could indicate important concerns of these children and may be relevant to their choice of silence as a way to be in school.

***

CHAPTER 15

Measuring change

In the initial StoryFrames research programme, with two children who had come from non-English speaking countries, the progress made after six weeks of this programme was remarkable. Both started talking to other children and joining in their games. Both were talking to and responding to their teachers.

Child A began initiating conversations with her teachers, joining in the play of other children, and showing her teacher her drawings. Her voice, which had started off being very quiet, was getting louder and more confident each week. This child's vocabulary and grammar also improved dramatically.

The other child, Child B, initially made a lot of progress in talking to teachers and children in the classroom, but after a while seemed to become slightly less outgoing, though he did continue speaking to teachers and to other children and was not by any means silent. On formal language tests it was seen that he had made the equivalent of six months of progress in vocabulary and grammar, during the six weeks of the programme (see Appendix II.) However he seemed to continue to have difficulty with turn-taking and would sometimes dominate a conversation.

It may be that this child would have benefited from participating in the programme for longer than the six weeks. He also seemed to be somewhat dysfluent at times; this was not consistent, and not very noticeable. It may have been a developmental stage he was going through; it may also have been that this dysfluency is what led to him being silent for so long. It was recommended that he should have a full assessment by a speech and language therapist, and that his teachers continue to monitor his language development.

In attempting to define the outcomes of a language programme for children in the Silent Period, we distinguish between qualitative and quantitative outcomes. For silent children, a standard type of language assessment is not an option: such a child will certainly not provide us with any sample of their spoken language to analyse, and they may not even want to participate in any activities which test their understanding of language. Of course, assessment in their home language would be ideal, but this is often not possible.

We need therefore to use qualitative outcomes, and try to measure change in their social and interactive behaviours, instead of looking at instances of language per se. This would include concepts which fall under the general heading of "the social use of language" (see Chapter Twelve above). What we are trying to measure seems rather difficult to define: in the words of Engel (1995) we are looking for evidence that the child feels "a robust sense of power and ownership, to feel that he can tell all kinds of stories to express all kinds of meanings".

How to record the outcomes of the programme

There is no set way to create this kind of qualitative assessment, because each silent child is so different in their presentation and behaviour. A teacher should feel free to list those aspects which are most worrying in the silent child's behaviour, and to monitor these behaviours over time. In addition, the person carrying out the StoryFrames programme with the child might, jointly with the teacher, come up with relevant items to monitor for any specific child.

In creating outcome measures it is necessary to observe the child before and after the programme. This observation must be carried out both in the classroom and in the playground, as well as during arrival and departure times. Any behaviours which cause concern, and any lack of expected social behaviours, should be listed.

Checklists for the social use of language

Examples of such items, which fall under the general heading of the social use of language, can be found in the two lists below. There is no need to use every item on these lists. The child's teacher should look through these lists and select those items which seem to be most relevant to each child.

The American Speech-Language-Hearing Association (ASHA) present the following useful list of the three major categories of skills involved in social communication.

ASHA: SKILLS IN SOCIAL COMMUNICATION

Using language for different reasons, such as
- Greeting (saying "Hello" or "Good-bye")
- Informing (saying "I'm going to get a cookie")
- Demanding (saying "Give me a cookie right now!")
- Promising (saying "I'm going to get you a cookie.")
- Requesting (saying "Can I have a cookie? or "I want a cookie")

Changing language for the listener or situation, such as
- Communicating differently to a baby than to a teacher or a friend
- Giving more information to someone who does not know the topic
- Knowing to skip some details when someone already knows the topic
- Communicating differently in a public place than at home

Following rules for conversations and storytelling, such as
- Taking turns being a talker and being a listener
- Letting others know the topic when you start talking
- Staying on topic
- Trying another way of saying what you mean when someone did not understand you
- Using gestures and body language, like pointing or shrugging
- Knowing how close to stand to someone when talking
- Using appropriate facial expressions and eye contact

https://www.asha.org/public/speech/development/social-communication/

Another excellent checklist is the Pragmatics Profile of Everyday Communication Skills in Children (Dewart and Summers 1995). The following list has been paraphrased from their list, and includes the items which are usually relevant specifically to the child in the Silent Period, but the entire Pragmatics Profile is worth reading in full.

> **PRAGMATICS PROFILE** (from Dewart and Summers 1995)
>
> **General communication skills**
> - Requesting objects
> - Requesting information or permission to do something
> - Rejecting, disagreeing or protesting
> - Greeting
> - Naming
> - Commenting on something seen or heard
> - Expressing feelings
> - Talking about past or future events
> - Giving information or explaining something
> - Expressing our wishes or intentions (I want to/ I would like to)
> - Asking other people to do something (will you....)
> - Giving one's own opinion
>
> **Interaction and conversation**
> - Calling a person by their name and making a request or asking them a question
> - Asking to join in a game
> - Asking for help if we have not understood what was said
> - Talking about a wide range of topics, for example toys, books, food
> - Taking more or less equal turns in a conversation instead of being a passive listener or dominating the conversation
> - Participating in games which involve role play and pretend play, with other children

A checklist can then be created by the child's class teacher. The checklist should be filled in by a member of staff who is not the person running the programme, as the person measuring the outcomes needs to be an objective observer.

When to complete the checklist

The checklist would be filled in on at least four occasions. The first time is, of course, just before the start of the programme, but subsequently it is important not only to fill in the checklist at the end of the programme but at other later time periods too. We are in this way making sure that the child maintains their progress over time. A reasonable time frame would be

- Just before the start of the programme
- Half way through the programme
- At the end of the programme
- One month after the end of the programme
- Three months after the end of the programme
- Six months after the end of the programme

The use of recorded transcripts of each session was necessary for the original research programme, but a teacher would not necessarily need these, and in fact this is an immensely time-consuming process. The measure of success is not what takes place in the actual StoryFrames sessions, but the changes seen in the child's behaviour in the classroom and in the playground.

The assessments used in the original research programme, with Children A and B, can be found in Appendix II below. They are rather different from the assessments recommended here, as they were used for the purposes of a research project, and are not recommended for use in the normal StoryFrames programme.

A teacher observation checklist for a specific child might therefore look something like the one below. Note that this is just an example, as each checklist must be specific to each child. Teachers should feel free to consult the published checklists above and to use the items which they feel are most relevant to the child in question.

TEACHER OBSERVATION CHECKLIST

NAME OF TEACHER .... NAME OF CHILD ....

	Responds to greeting from the teacher when entering the class	Uses gesture and pointing to express a wish or idea	Takes turns in a short conversation	Joins in with other children in play in small groups, but without speaking	Asks other children if she may join in their game	Replies when asked a yes/no question by a teacher	Talks to other children while playing with them
Date of observation (Start of programme)							
Date of observation (Half way through programme)							
Date of observation (End of programme)							
Date of observation (1 month after end of programme)							
Date of observation (3 months after end of programme)							
Date of observation (6 months after end of programme)							

***

A brief note about what we do *not* measure in the StoryFrames programme

- **Speech (the speech sounds of a language)**

Most children learn some of the speech sounds of their own language later than other speech sounds; this is part of the normal acquisition of language. However, some struggle to speak in a way which is clearly intelligible to others, even when speaking their home language. Other people, who speak the home language of the child, might say that they do not understand what the child is saying. In this case, speech and language therapy might be indicated.

If it is the case that the child's speech is *not understood in their own (home) language*, please refer the child to speech and language therapy.

There may well be, in the new language which the child needs to learn, some speech sounds which do not exist in their home language. (For example, the 'th' sound in English is one of the sounds which does not exist in many other languages.) However the StoryFrames programme is not concerned with the speech sounds being used by the child. Our aim is for the child to develop an ability to communicate their wishes, feelings and needs to others; to be able to use language socially. A few unusual-sounding speech sounds are not relevant at this stage in the child's life.

- **Language (vocabulary and grammar, understanding and speaking)**

There are distinct stages in which a young child learning a home language develops an understanding of words and grammar, and learns to use words and grammar in their speech. The table in Appendix III provides a very general outline of these stages.

Please note however that the information in the table in Appendix III refers to the development of a child's *home language*, and does not apply to the learning of a second language. The table is provided merely as a reference, to give readers some idea of the various aspects of language which are relevant in a child's development.

The StoryFrames programme, as described above, aims to enable the child to communicate with others, to interact and play with the other children in the school, freely and comfortably. It is not a language development programme, nor is it a programme to teach a second language. The focus of the StoryFrames programme is not on *how* the child speaks, but *that* the child speaks and interacts.

So even though in the original research, measures of the children's vocabulary and language were carried out, this was only for the purpose of the research, and is not part of the StoryFrames programme. As we have said repeatedly, the focus of this programme is the social and interactive use of language. Of course language is required for this, and children who participate in this programme do almost always make significant progress in their spoken vocabulary and grammar, but that is not the main focus of the programme.

If you are in doubt, or if you are concerned that your child has a speech and/or language delay *in their home language*, you should consult a speech and language therapist.

***

CHAPTER 16

Endings

This book is essentially a manual explaining how to carry out the StoryFrames programme, through which we enable children to emerge from the Silent Period, to interact with others and to use language socially.

In the original research, with Child A and Child B, the measure of the success of the original StoryFrames programme was whether the children became more active and confident communicators, with both peers and teachers. In the case of both of these children, the programme achieved its aims and the children emerged from their silence within a period of six weeks. In this short time it was heart-warming to witness them developing their sense of agency: the sense of themselves as people who are able to communicate their ideas and feelings to others, to ask questions, and to play with other children.

As Hoffman says (2008) moving to a new country and a new language requires us not only to learn a new word but also to learn a whole new world. The experience of running this programme with children in the Silent Period shows us how much can be gained for the child from this kind of individual support, but also brings home how much they may have lost: their previous surroundings, friends they may previously have known, and the ability to use their language, without effort or conscious thought, in order to live in the world.

As we have said, this programme is not a programme to teach English as a second language; it is a programme to support the silent child to be able to interact socially and communicatively with other people at school. However, the gains these two children made in their spoken English were remarkable (see Appendix II).

An unexpected benefit of the original research programme was that the teachers at the school became interested, after seeing the progress of these two children, in the way the programme is run. Some began to incorporate some of the ideas in their daily teaching and also came up with useful strategies for these children.

For more information, or if you have any questions about the programme, please feel free to contact the author at cynthia@cynthiapelman.com

***

This final transcript is from a session at the end of the StoryFrames programme with Child B. Please note that even though we are now in the Expanding stage of the programme, all the other strategies (Feelings, Repeating, Adding and Modelling) are still being used as and when they are felt to be needed.

We will let one of the previously silent children have the last word:

Speaker	Transcript	Strategy
	[Child B chooses a well-known picture book which he has seen previously, both in his classroom and in the StoryFrames sessions. He is clearly familiar with the story, which is about a caterpillar who eats, grows and is transformed (Carle 1969).]	
TEACHER	Can you tell me the story?	M: Modelling story structure
CHILD B	[pointing to picture] Egg.	
TEACHER	And then?	E: Expanding
CHILD B	[Child B turns the pages very quickly to get through to the end] He's want to eat the [unintelligible]	
TEACHER	He wants to eat	R: Repeating
CHILD B	He very hungry	
TEACHER	He's very hungry	R: Repeating
CHILD B	And he's eat apple [the child turns the page] and he's eat pear... pear [turns page] and he's eat two more pear on this side [The child points to the reverse page] He's [unintelligible] This one, this one, he's tooken [sic] off that one...	
TEACHER	And then? What did he do? [The teacher points to the picture]	E: Expanding
CHILD B	He's took [sic] all the strawberry and the orange and he's eaten cake and - and lollipop and ... [pause] and melon and the.... [pause] that don't look like... [pause] like cake and melon! [Loud voice]	The child tells a story which follows a sequence in time
CHILD B	[Turning more pages] And he's eat all the leaf up there. [sic]	
TEACHER	And then? [The teacher turns the page and points to the salient parts of the picture]	E: Expanding
CHILD B	He's grow! [Very loud voice]	
TEACHER	Yes, he's grown. And then?	R: Repeating E: Expanding
CHILD B	He's turn into a butterfly!	
TEACHER	He's turned into a butterfly. What a beautiful butterfly! The end.	R: Repeating E: Expanding M: Modelling story structure (an ending)
CHILD B	The end.	Traditional Story Grammar ending

BIBLIOGRAPHY

Aho, K. (2010) The psychopathology of American shyness: A hermeneutic reading. *Journal for the Theory of Social Behavior.* (40) pp 190-202

Alexander, R. J. (1995/2003) Talk in teaching and learning: international perspectives. In *New Perspectives on spoken English in the classroom: discussion papers.* Qualifications and Curriculum Authority (QCA) (2003) National Curriculum:

Alexander, R.J. (2004) *Towards Dialogic Teaching: rethinking classroom talk.* Dialogos

Amer, A. (1992) The effect of story grammar instruction on EFL students' comprehension of narrative text. *Reading in a Foreign Language.* Vol.8 (2) pp 711- 720.

Ameka, F.K and Breedveld, A. (2004) Area cultural scripts for social interaction in West African communities. *Intercultural Pragmatics.* Vol. 1 (2) pp 167-187

Applebee, A. (1978) *The Child's concept of story: ages two to seventeen.* Chicago, Illinois: University of Chicago Press.

Arizpe, E., Colomer, T. and Martinez-Roldan, C. (2014) *Visual Journeys through wordless narratives: an International Inquiry with Immigrant Children and* The Arrival. Bloomsbury.

Aron, E.N., Aron, A., Jagiellowicz, J. (2012) Sensory Processing Sensitivity: A review in the Light of the Evolution of Biological Responsivity. *Personality and Social Psychology Review*, Vol. 16 (3) https://doi.org/10.1177/1088868311434213

Aron, E. N. (2002) *The Highly Sensitive Child: Helping our children thrive when the world overwhelms them.* Harper Collins Publishers.

Asher, J. (2009) *Learning Another Language through Actions.* Sky Oak Productions; 7th edition

Baker, S.T., Le Courtois, S., Eberhart, J. (2021) Making space for children's agency with playful learning. *International Journal of Early Years Education.* Routledge. https://doi.org/10.1080/09669760.2021.1997726 [Accessed online 26.4.2023]

Bandura, A. (1977) *Social Learning Theory.* Prentice-Hall Series in Social Learning.

Bakhtin, M.M. (1981) *The Dialogic Imagination.* Austin, Texas: University of Texas

Barnes, E., Puccioni, J. (2017) *Shared book reading and preschool children's academic achievement: Evidence from the Early Childhood Longitudinal Study—Birth cohort* https://doi.org/10.1002/icd.2035

Barnes, H.E. (1997)*The Story I tell Myself.* University of Chicago.

Baumeiseter, R.F. and Leary M.R. (1995) The Need to Belong: Desire for interpersonal attachments as a fundamental human motivation. *Psychological Bulletin.* 117 (3) pp 497-529.

Birckmayer, J., Kennedy, A., Stonehouse, A. (2009) Using Stories Effectively with Infants and Toddlers. *Young Children.* 64 (1) Jan 2009 pp 42-47

Bishop, D.V.M. and Edmundsen A. (1987) Specific Language Impairment as a maturational lag: Evidence from longitudinal data on language and motor development. *Developmental Medicine and Child Neurology.* (29) pp 442-459

Blank, M. & Sheila, J. (1986) Questions: A Powerful but Misused Form of Classroom Exchange. *Topics in Language Disorders*, 6(2) pp 1-12.

Bligh, C. (2011) (Unpublished Doctoral Thesis) *The Silent Experiences of Young Bilingual Learners: A small Scale Sociocultural Exploration.* CREET: The Open University.

Boyce, W.T. (2019) *The Orchid and the Dandelion: Why Some Children Struggle and How All Can Thrive.* Knopf.

Boyd, B. (2005) Evolutionary Theories of Art. In *The Literary Animal.* Gottshall. J. and Wilson, D.S. Northwestern University Press.

Boyd, B. (2009) *On the Origin of Stories.* Harvard University Press

Broadhead, P. (2004) *Early Years Play and Learning: developing social skills and cooperation.* London: Routledge/Falmer

Brooker, L. (2002) *Starting School: Young Children Learning Cultures.* McGraw-Hill Education

Brown, A. (2022) Social Anxiety? Introvert? Or Shy? In *Mind Journal* https://commons.wikimedia.org/wiki/File:20220801_Introversion_-_Shyness_-_Social_anxiety_disorder_-_comparative_chart.svg [accessed online 17.3.2013]

Brown, J. M., & Palmer, A. S. (1988) *The Listening Approach: Methods and Materials for Applying Krashen's Input Hypothesis.* Longman.

Bruner, J.S. (1986) *Actual Minds, Possible Worlds.* Cambridge, Mass: Harvard University Press

Byers-Heinlein, K. and Lew-Williams, C. (2013) Bilingualism in the Early Years: What the Science Says. *Learning Landscape,* Autumn, Vol. 7 (1) pp 95-112

Caldwell, P. (2002) *Learning the Language.* Brighton: Pavilion Publishing

Campbell, J. and Moyers, B. (1988) *The Power of Myth.* New York: Doubleday Dell Publishing.

Carle, E. (1969) *The Very Hungry Caterpillar.* World Publishing Company (US) Hamish Hamilton (UK)

Cattanach, A. (2008) *Narrative Approaches in Play with Children.* Jessica Kingsley Publishers.

Chen, X., Rubin, K. H., & Sun, Y. (1992) Social reputation and peer relationships in Chinese and Canadian children: A cross-cultural study. *Child Development,* 63(6), pp1336-1341 https://doi.org/10.2307/1131559

Clarke, P. (1992) *English as a Second Language in Early Childhood.* FKA Multicultural Resource Centre, Victoria, Australia.

Clarke, P. (1997) *Principles of second language learning.* Unpublished paper, FKA Multicultural Resource Centre, Melbourne, Victoria, Australia.

Cordier, R., Speyer, R., Mahoney, N., Arnesen, A., Mjelve, L.M., Nyborg, G. (2021) Effects of interventions for social anxiety and shyness in school-aged children: A systematic review and meta-analysis. *PLoS One.* 2021; 16(7): e0254117. [Published online 2021. Accessed 28.3.2023]

Craib, I. (1994) *The Importance of Disappointment.* Routledge.

Cummins, J. (1981) *Bilingualism and Minority Language Children*: Toronto: Ontario Institute for Studies in Education.

Dangmann, C., Dybdahl, R., Solberg, O. (2022) Mental Health in Refugee Children. *Current Opinions in Psychology,* Vol. 48.

Danon-Boileau, L. (2001) *The Silent Child: exploring the world of children who do not speak.* Oxford University Press.

Da Silva, I.A. and McCafferty, S. (2007) *Carnival in a mainstream kindergarten classroom: A Bakhtinian analysis of language learners' off-task behaviours.* The Modern Language Journal, (91) pp 31-44

Dewart, H. and Summers, S. (1995) *The Pragmatics Profile of Everyday Communication Skills in Children* (Revised Edition) [Accessed online 30.04.2023]

Doey, L., Coplan, R.J. & Kingsbury, M. (2014) Bashful Boys and Coy Girls: A Review of Gender Differences in Childhood Shyness. In *Feminist Forum*. Sex Roles. Vol. 70, pp 255–266.

Donald, M. (1991) *Origins of the Modern Mind: Three Stages in the Evolution of Culture and Cognition.* Harvard University Press

Donaldson, M. (1992) *Human Minds: An Exploration.* New York: Allen Lane.

Drury, R. (2007) *Young bilingual learners at Home and School: researching multilingual voices.* Stoke-On-Trent: Trentham Books

Ellis, B.J., James, J., and Boyce, W.T. (2006) The stress response systems: Universality and adaptive individual differences. *Developmental Review*, Vol. 26 (2) pp 175-212 DOI: 10.1016/j.dr.2006.02.004

Engel, S. (1995) *The Stories Children Tell.* New York: W. H. Freeman and Co.

Engel, S. (2016) *Storytelling in the First Three Years.* Washington, DC: Zero to Three. [Accessed 14.06.2023] www.zerotothree.org/resources/1057-storytelling-in-the-first-three-years

Fabian, H. and Mou, C. (2009) *Development and Learning for Very Young Children.* London: Sage

Feuerstein R. And Fallik L. (2015) *Changing Children's Minds – The Legacy of Reuven Feuerstein; Higher Thinking and Cognition through Mediated Learning.* Teachers College Press, Columbia University.

Forbes, R. (2004) *Beginning to Play: Young Children from Birth to Three.* Open University Press.

Fivush, R. (2022) *Autobiographical Memory and Narrative in Childhood.* Cambridge University Press.

Frederickson, B. (2002) Positive emotions. In Snyder, C.R. and Lopez, S.J (Eds.) *Handbook of Positive Psychology.* New York: Oxford University Press

Freud, S. and Breuer, J. (1895/ 2004) Translated by Nicola Luckhurst. *Studies in Hysteria.* London 2004. ISBN 978-0-141-18482-1)

Gaab, C. (2021) *Language Magazine* www.languagemagazine.com [accessed online 21.3.2023] For a detailed example of a TPRS lesson structure, please refer to https://www.languagemagazine.com/multistory-construction/#:~:text=TPRS%20(Teaching%20Proficiency%20through%20Reading,comprehensible%2C%20personalized%20and%20contextualized%20manner.

Gardner R.C. and MacIntyre, P.D. (1993) *A student's contributions to second language learning.* Part II: affective variables. Language Teaching. (26) pp 1-11

Garvie, E. (1990) *Story as Vehicle: Teaching English to Young Children.* Philadelphia: Multilingual Matters.

Ghalebi, R. and Sadighi, F. (2015) The Usage-based Theory of Language Acquisition: A review of Major Issues. *Journal of Applied Linguistics and Language Research* Vol. 2 (6) pp 190-195

Gibson, J.J. (1979/ 2014) *The Ecological Approach to Visual Perception.* Psychology Press & Routledge Classic Editions

Gleitman, L., & Papafragou, A. (2005) Language and thought. In K. Holyoak & R. Morrison (Eds.), *Cambridge handbook of thinking and reasoning* pp. 633–661. Cambridge, UK: Cambridge University Press.

Gleitman, L. R., & Papafragou, A. (2016) New perspectives on language and thought. In K. Holyoak & R. Morrison (Eds.), *The Oxford handbook of Thinking and Reasoning* pp 543-568 (2nd ed.) New York: Oxford University Press.

Gotschall, J. (2013) *The Storytelling Animal: How Stories made us Human*. Boston: First Mariner Books.

Granger, C.A. (2004). *Silence in Second Language Learning: A Psychoanalytic Reading*. Multilingual Matters.

Gregory, J. (2002) Principles of experiential education. In P. Jarvis (Ed.) *The theory & practice of teaching: School and beyond in the learning society* (pp 94-107). New York: Routledge. (2nd ed.)

Hall, K. M., Sabey, B. L. & McClellan, M. (2005) Expository text comprehension: Helping primary-grade teachers use expository texts to full advantage. *Reading Psychology*, 26, pp 211-234.

Heath, S.B. (1985) Narrative Play in Second Language Learning. In *Play, Language and Behaviour: the development of children's literate behaviours*. Galda, L. and Pellegrini, A.D. (Eds.) Norwood NJ: Ablex

Hirsch-Pasek, K., and Golinkoff, R.M. (2011) The Great Balancing Act: Optimising core curricula through playful pedagogy. In *The Pre-K debates: Current controversies and Issues*. Zigler, E., Gilliam W.S., and Barnett W.S. (Eds.) pp 110-116. Baltimore, MD: Brooked Publishing Co.

Hoffman, E. (2008) *Lost in Translation: life in a new language*. Minerva

Hoffman S.G. and DiBartolo P.M. (Eds.) (2014) *Social Anxiety: Clinical, Developmental and Social Perspectives* (3rd Ed). Elsevier.

Hofstadter, D. R and Sander, E. (2013) *Surfaces and Essences: Analogy as the Fuel and Fire of Thinking*. Basic Books.

Houston, M. and Kramarae, C. (1991) Women Speaking from Silence: methods of silencing and resistance. *Discourse and Society*, Vol. 2, (4) pp 387-399

Hoy, R.R. (1993) A 'Model Minority' Speaks Out on Cultural Shyness. *Science*, Vol. 262, pp1117-1118 (November) doi: 10.1126/science.262.5136.1117.

Hunter, J. (1997) *Multiple perceptions: social identity in a multilingual elementary classroom*. TESOL Quarterly 31, pp 603-611

James, W. (1890/ 1983) *The Principles of Psychology, Volumes I and II*. Cambridge, MA: Harvard University Press

Jang, H., Reeve J., and Deci E. (2010) Engaging students in learning activities: It is not autonomy, support or structure but autonomy, support and structure. *Journal of Educational Psychology* 102 (3) p. 588.

Jarman, E. *The Communication Friendly Spaces Toolkit: Improving Speaking and Listening Skills in the Early Years Foundation Stage*. www.elizabethjarmanltd.co.uk/store www.elizabethjarman.com [accessed online 14.3.2023]

Jeffrey, B and Craft, A. (2004) Teaching creatively and teaching for creativity: distinctions and relationships. *Educational Studies*, Vol. 30 (1)

Joanisse, M. and McClelland J.L. (2105) Connectionist perspectives on language learning, representation and processing. *Wiley Interdisciplinary Review Cogn Sci* May-Jun; 6(3) pp 235-47.

Johnson, M. and Wintgens, A. (2016) The Selective Mutism Resource Manual. Speechmark

Kagan, J. (1989) The concept of behavioural inhibition to the unfamiliar. In Reznick, J. (Ed.) *Perspectives on Behavioural Inhibition*. pp 1-23. Chicago: The University of Chicago Press.

Krashen, S. (1981) *Second Language Acquisition and Second Language Learning*. Oxford: Pergamon

Krashen, S. D., & Terrell, T. D. (1983) *The Natural Approach: Language Acquisition in the Classroom*. Hemel Hempstead: Prentice Hall International English Language Teaching.

Kuczaj, S. (1982) Language Play and Language acquisition. *Advances in Child Development and Behaviour,* (17) pp 198-232.

Lave, J. And Wenger, E. (1991) *Situated learning: Legitimate Peripheral Participation.* Cambridge: Cambridge University Press.

Le Courtois, S. and Baker, S. How Montessori, Reggio Emilia and Mantle of the Expert support children's agency in their learning. *Early Childhood Hub.* https://my.chartered.college/early-childhood-hub/how-montessori-reggio-emilia-and-mantle-of-the-expert-support-childrens-agency-in-their-learning/ [Accessed online 08.05.2023]

Lewis, M. (1995) *Shame: The Exposed Self.* New York: The Free Press

Lewis, M. (1999) Social cognition and the self. In Rochat, P. (Ed.) *Early Social Cognition: Understanding others in the first months of life.* Mahwah, N.J: Lawrence Erlbaum Associates.

Lichtman, K. (2018) *TPRS: an input-based approach to second language instruction.* Routledge

Little, D. (1991) *Learner Autonomy I: Definition, Issues and problems.* Dublin: Authentik.

Long, M. (1981) Input, interaction and second language acquisition. In Winitz, H. (Ed.) *Native Language and Foreign Language Acquisition.* pp 259-278 Annals of the New York Academy of Sciences

Manyukhina, Y. and Wyse, D. (2021) *Children's agency: What is it, and what should be done?* British Educational Research Association (BERA) Blog [accessed online 21.04.2023]

Marsten, D., Epston, D., and Markham, L. (2016) *Narrative Therapy in Wonderland: Connecting with Children's Imaginative Know-How.* W. W. Norton & Company

Martin, B.J and Carle, E. (1996) *Brown Bear, Brown Bear, What do you See?* New York, Henry Holt and Co.

McCabe, A. (1997) Developmental and Cross-cultural aspects of children's narratives. In Bamberg, M. *Narrative Development: Six Approaches.* pp 137-174. Mahwah, NJ: Lawrence Erlbaum Assoc.

McGregor, K. K. (2020) How We Fail Children With Developmental Language Disorder. *Language, Speech and Hearing Services in Schools,* (51) pp 981-992

Morgan, A. (2000) *What is Narrative Therapy? An easy-to-read introduction.* Dulwich Centre Publications.

Nadel, J., (2002) Imitation and imitation recognition: Functional use in preverbal infants and nonverbal children with autism. In Meltzoff, A. and Prinz, W. (Eds.) *The imitative mind: development, evolution and brain bases* Cambridge: Cambridge University Press

Nelson, K. (1996) *Language in Cognitive Development: The Emergence of the Mediated Mind.* Cambridge University Press.

Nelson, K., and Fivush, R. (2020) The development of autobiographical memory, autobiographical narratives, and autobiographical consciousness. *Psychological Reports, 123*(1), pp 71–96. https://doi.org/10.1177/0033294119852574

Nicolopoulou, A. (1997) Children and narratives: Toward an interpretive and sociocultural approach. In Bamberg, M. (Ed.) *Narrative Development: Six Approaches.* (Chapter 5) Mahwah, NJ. Lawrence Erlbaum associates

Ntuli, C. (2012) Intercultural misunderstanding in South Africa: An analysis of nonverbal communication behaviour in context. *Intercultural Communication Studies.* Vol. 21 (22) pp 20-31

Omar, A. (1991) How learners greet in Kiswahili: A cross-sectional survey. In Bouton, L.F. and Kachru, Y. (Eds.) *Pragmatics and Language Learning.* pp 59-73. University of Illinois.

Paley, V.G. (1981) *Wally's Stories.* Harvard University Press.

Paley, V.G. (1990) *The Boy who would be a Helicopter.* Harvard University Press.

Parke. T., and Drury, R. (2001) Language development at home and school: gains and losses in young bilinguals. *Early Years: An International Journal of Research and Development,* 21 (2) pp 117- 127

Pegg, L.A, and Bartelheim, F.J. (2011) Effects of daily read-alouds on students' sustained silent reading. *Current Issues in Education,* 14 (2).

Pellegrini, A. (1985) The relations between symbolic play and literate behaviour: a review and critique of the empirical literature. *Review of Educational Research* (55) pp 107-121

Perry, N.E. (2013) Understanding Classroom Practices that support children's self-regulation of learning. In BJEP Monograph Series II: Part 10. *Self-regulation and Dialogue in Primary Classrooms.* Whitebread, D., Mercer, N., Howe, C. and Tolmie, A. (Eds.) pp 45-67. Leicester: British Psychological Society.

Peterson, A.L., (2019) Introversion, Shyness and Social Anxiety: What's the Difference? *Mental Health at Home,* https://mentalhealthathome.org/2019/04/11/introversion-shyness-anxiety/ [accessed online 17.3.2013]

Peterson, C. and McCabe, A. (1983) *Developmental Psycholinguistics: Three ways of looking at a child's narrative.* New York: Plenum

Philp, J. Oliver, R. and Mackey, A. (2008) (Eds.) *Second Language Acquisition and the Younger Learner.* John Benjamin Publishing Company.

Piaget, J. (1954) *The construction of reality in the child* (New York: Basic Books) [*La construction du réel chez l'enfant* (1950), also translated as *The Child's Construction of Reality.* London: Routledge and Kegan Paul, 1955.

Piaget, J. (1972) *Psychology and Epistemology: Towards a Theory of Knowledge.* Harmondsworth: Penguin.

Prior, M., Smart, D., Sansom, A., Oberklaid, F. (2000) Does shy-inhibited temperament in childhood lead to anxiety problems in adolescence? *J Am Acad Child Adolesc Psychiatry.* Vol. 39 (4) pp 461-8.

Ray, B. and Seely, C. (2004) *Fluency Through TPR Storytelling: Achieving Real Language Acquisition in School* (4th ed.). Command Performance Language Institute, Blaine Ray Workshops.

Reddy, V. (2008) *How Infants know Minds.* Harvard University Press, Cambridge.

Renfrew Language Scales (1997) *Action Picture Test and Bus Story Test.* Winslow Press.

Roberts, T.A. (2014) Not so silent after all: Examination and analysis of the silent stage in childhood second language acquisition. *Early Childhood Research Quarterly,* 29 (1) pp 22-40

Rogers, C. (1956) *Client-Centered Therapy* (3rd ed.). Boston: Houghton-Mifflin.

Rogoff, B. (2003) *The Cultural Nature of Human Development.* New York: Oxford University Press.

Roskos, K. (1990) *A taxonomic view of pretend play activity among 4- and 5-year olds.* Early Childhood Research Quarterly, 5, pp 495-512

Rudasill, K.M., Rimm-Kaufman, S.E. (2009) Teacher-child relationship quality: the roles of child temperament and teacher-child interactions. *Early Childhood Research Quarterly,* (24) pp 107-120

Rumelhart, D.E. (1980) On Evaluating Story Grammars. *Cognitive Science* (4) pp 313-316.

Saville-Troike, M. (1998) Private speech: Evidence for second language learning strategies, during the "silent period". *Journal of Child Language.* 15 (3): pp 567–590.

Scott, S. (2006) The medicalisation of shyness: from social misfits to social fitness. In *Sociology of Health and Illness*, Vol. 28 (2) pp 133-153

Schegloff, E.A. (2000) Overlapping Talk and the Organization of Turn-Taking for Conversation. *Language in Society*, Vol.29 (1) pp 1-63

Sfard, A. (1998) On Two Metaphors for Learning and the Dangers of Choosing Just One. *Educational Researcher* (27) pp. 4-13

Shaik, N. (2015) Why children should be seen and heard in school. https://www.weforum.org/agenda/2015/06/why-children-should-be-seen-and-heard-in-school/ [retrieved online 16.3.2023]

Smuts, B. (2001) Encounters with Animal Minds. *Journal of Consciousness Studies*, (8) pp 293-309

SMIRA (2012) Selective Mutism Information and Research Association (SMIRA) [accessed online 14.03.2023] www.selectivemutism.org.uk

Snow, C. and Ninio, A. (1992) The Contracts of Literacy: what children can learn from learning to read books. In Teale, W.H. and Sulzby, E. *Emergent Literacy: writing and reading*. Norwood: Ablex

Sommer, G. and Lapapula, A. (2012) Comparing address forms and systems: some examples from Bantu, In Marlo, M. et al (Eds.) *Selected Proceedings of the 42nd annual conference on African Linguistics.* pp 266-277

Spence, S.H. and Rapee, R.M. (2016) The etiology of social anxiety disorder: An evidence-based model. *Behaviour Research and Therapy*,(86) November, pp 50-67

Sperber, D. and Wilson, D. (1995) *Relevance: Communication and Cognition*. 2nd Edition, Blackwell Publishing.

Stein, N. & Glenn, C. (1979) An analysis of story comprehension in elementary school children. In R. D. Freedle (Ed.), *Advances in discourse processes: Vol. 2. New directions in discourse processing.* pp 53-119. Norwood, NJ: Ablex.

Stern, D. (2004) *The present moment in psychotherapy and everyday life*. New York: W.W. Norton and Co.

Sugimura, N. (2018) *What Makes Youth More Likely to Be Bullied?* https://www.publichealthpost.org/research/youth-more-likely-to-be-bullied/ [accessed online 19.3.2023]

Swain, M. (2001) The Output Hypothesis and Beyond: Mediating acquisition through collaborative dialogue. In Lantolf, J.P. (Ed.) *Sociocultural Theory and Second Language Learning.* pp 97-114. Oxford: Oxford University Press

Swain, M. and Lapkin, S. (2002) Oh I get it now. From production to comprehension in second language learning. In Brinton, D.M. and Kagan, O. (Eds.) *Heritage Language Acquisition: a new field emerging*. Mahwah, NJ: Lawrence Erlbaum

Symeonidou, S. and Loizou, E. (2023) Bridging early childhood education and inclusive practices in classrooms that serve children with disabilities: a narrative portrait. *European Early Childhood Education Research Journal*, Vol 31 (1) pp 92-105. The inclusion of children with disabilities in Early Childhood. https://doi.org/10.1080/1350293X.2022.2140817 [accessed online 18.07.2023]

Tabors, P.O. (Ed.) (2008) *One Child, Two Languages*: A *Guide for Early Childhood Educators of Children Learning English as a Second Language.* (2nd Edition) Baltimore, MD. Paul H. Brookes.

Tagore, R. (1894/1985) Broken Song. *Selected Poems*. Penguin.

Tan, S. (2009) Illustration and Visual Narrative. https://www.shauntan.net/essay-colin-simpson accessed online 23.06.2023]

Tannen, D. and Saville-Troike, M. (1985) *Perspectives on Silence*. Norwood NJ: Ablex

Taylor, T. (2016) *A beginner's guide to Mantle of the Expert*. Singular Publishing

Thompson, K.L., Hannan, S.M., Miron, L.R. (2014) Fight, flight, and freeze: Threat sensitivity and emotion dysregulation in survivors of chronic childhood maltreatment. *Personality and Individual Differences*, Vol. 69, October, pp. 28-32.

Tomasello, M. (2003) *Constructing a language: A usage-based theory of language acquisition*. Harvard University Press.

Tomasello, M. (2019) *Becoming human: a theory of ontogeny*. Belknap Press of Harvard University Press.

Tomasello, M. (2022) *The Evolution of Agency: Behavioural Organization from Lizards to Humans*. MIT Press

Toohey, K. and Norton, B. (2001) *Changing Perspectives on good language learners*. TESOL Quarterly (35) pp 307-22

Tovey, H. (2007) *Playing outdoors: spaces and places, risk and challenge*. Maidenhead: Open University Press

Vygotsky, L. (1978) *Mind in Society: The development of Higher Psychological Processes*. Cambridge: Harvard University Press.

Vygotsky, L. (1986) *Thought and Language*. In Kozulin, A. (Translated and Edited) *Thought and Language*. Cambridge, MA: MIT Press

Vygotsky, L. (2023) *Play And its Role in The Mental Development of The Child* (Psychology Classics Book 1) www.all-about-psychology.com. [accessed online 13.06.2023]

Wells, G. (1985) *The Meaning Makers*. Portsmouth: Heinemann

Wenger, E. (1998) *Communities of Practice: Learning, Meaning and Identity*. Cambridge: Cambridge University Press.

Wenger, E. and Nuckles, M. (2013) Knowledge acquisition or participation in communities of practice? Academics' metaphors of teaching and learning at the university. *Studies in Higher Education* pp 624-643

Whitehead, M. (2002) Dylan's Route to Literacy. The First Three Years with Picture Books. *Journal of Early Childhood Literacy*, Vol. 2 (3)

Whitehurst, G.J., Falco, F.L., Lonigan, C.J., Fischel, J.E., De Baryshe B.D., Valdez-Menchaca, M.C., and Caulfield, M. (1988) *Accelerating language development through picture book reading*. Developmental Psychology Vol. 24, pp 552-559

Winnicott, D.W. (1957) *The Child and the Outside World*. Tavistock

Winnicott, D.W. (2018) *The Maturational Processes and the Facilitating Environment: Studies in the Theory of Emotional Development*. Routledge

Wood, D., Bruner, J. and Ross, G. (1976) *The Role of Tutoring in Problem Solving*. J. Child Psychology and Psychiatry, (17) pp 89-100

Yamamoto, Y. and Li, J. (2011) Is being quiet a virtue or a problem? Implications of a study on Chinese immigrant children in the U.S. *Child Research Net*. https://www.childresearch.net/papers/multi/2011_01.html [accessed online 23.3.2023]

Zeedyk, S. (2006) From intersubjectivity to subjectivity: the transformative roles of emotional intimacy and imitation. *Infant and Child Development*, (15) pp 321-344

Zimbardo, P.G. (1977) *Shyness: what it is, what to do about it*. Reading, MA: Addison-Wesley

***

APPENDIX I

Quick Reference: A summary of the StoryFrames programme

This is a brief summary of the main stages and strategies in the StoryFrames programme.

EQUIPMENT	➢ **Miniature world toys** See list in Chapter Five ➢ **Picture books** A selection of favourite picture books, both fiction and non-fiction. See ideas for reading aloud in Chapter Five ➢ **Stationery** Post-it notes, paper, card, scissors, glue, stapler, pencils, to make your own books
SPACE	A quiet enclosed space, away from the classroom if possible
TIME	20-30 minutes uninterrupted time, once or twice a week, for about 6 weeks.
WHAT YOU DO	• Work in a quiet and secluded space • Sit next to the child • Offer the child the toys and let the child choose what they want to do • Offer to read to the child from a picture book. • Let the child play while you watch attentively • Start making up a story based on the child's play • Re-tell and write down the story • Help the child tell the story • Write down the child's story and make a book to give to the child
WHAT YOU SAY The F.R.A.M.E STAGES AND STRATEGIES	• Sharing the feelings (F) which emerge either verbally or non-verbally: (Oh dear! Oh no!) Use your facial expressions to show interest and empathy • Repeat (R): Repeat the child's sounds, words and exclamations to show you are listening and that their words and sounds matter to you • Add words (A): Describe what the child is doing; put the child's play into words using simple short sentences • Model (M): Model story structures using Story Grammar (e.g. once upon a time/ and then... and then... the end.) • Expanding (E): Expand the play if too repetitive, by adding a new toy; expand the story being told by adding your own ideas, comments, and expanding the language you use in re-telling the child's story.
TIPS	• Don't be surprised if the child enacts the same scenes over and over • Don't be surprised if most of the play and stories are violent or scary (death, monsters, car crashes, police, desperate situations) • At the end of the session, retell the story that the child has pretend-played • Pack the kit away by placing the toys in their allotted space; storing it safely so that it is kept only for these sessions.

APPENDIX II

Language assessments used in the research project

This section presents, for anyone wishing to find out more about the original research project, the speech and language assessments used with the two children before and after their participation in the programme.

This is not to suggest that running the StoryFrames programme requires access to or use of such assessments. The description of how to measure outcomes in Chapter 15 above (Measuring Change) is all that is needed for the programme.

The initial research was carried out by the author, a speech and language therapist. The two children who took part in the original research study were assessed with two brief language assessments commonly used in the United Kingdom: the Action Picture Test and the Bus Story Test from the Renfrew Language Scales (Renfrew 1997). Both children were assessed before and after the programme.

In addition, several hours of observation were carried out, both in the classroom and in the playground, by the speech therapist and by their teachers. The class teachers and the children's parents were interviewed to get as much information as possible about the children's language and social interaction at home and at school.

Of course, interpreting the formal speech and language test results was challenging due to the children's preference for silence. An assessment of spoken language would clearly not be able to be used in any reliable way. There was also found to be a significant difference in the language output these children used in class as opposed to when they were in the secluded space away from the classroom; they seemed to feel much freer to speak in the secluded space. For this reason, any assessment carried out in the secluded space, away from the classroom, might not be fully representative of these children's daily communication levels. And indeed, during the pre-programme assessments, which were carried out in a quiet secluded space, these two children were found to be much more verbal than they had been in all of their months at school.

A decision to minimise the use of formal standardised assessments was made, and observation and informal assessment were preferred. It was felt that in view of the long-lasting silence of these two children, the priority was intervention, rather than further assessment.

The teacher interviews before and after the StoryFrames programme were of great value in assessing the progress made. A simple table was used (see Appendix III) which categorises four important aspects of communication: attention and listening, understanding of language, spoken language (including speech sounds, vocabulary and sentences) and social interaction and play (the social use of language in interaction with others.) This was completed by the child's class teacher.

As we have said, the main aim of the programme is not to teach English, but rather to give the children the confidence to use their voices, and to interact and play with other children. Of course spoken language is one way, and the most efficient way, to interact communicatively, but this is not the prime motivation for the programme. Gains in vocabulary and syntax are therefore seen as a benefit, but not as the main intention.

The formal assessments used in the research

The Action Picture Test comprises 10 simple coloured illustrations of a person or animal carrying out an activity. The child is asked a simple question, such as "what is the person doing?" and the answer is written down on the score sheet. The Action Picture Test scores, when used for a home-language English speaker, would give an age- equivalent language level for both vocabulary and grammar; when used for these non-home-language English speakers, it was only possible to compare their pre-programme results (number of points gained for vocabulary and for grammar) with their post-programme results, without translating the scores into age-equivalent levels.

The Bus Story Test consists of a short story about a bus which runs away from its driver and has some adventures. The assessor tells the story in full to the child, while pointing to each picture in turn. The child is then asked to re-tell the story, while the assessor again points to the pictures. The responses are then scored for vocabulary, sentence length and for the presence of subordinate clauses. In a well-known research programme, The Bus Story Test when used with home-language English speaking children aged 4 was found to be a reliable predictor of later language development (Bishop and Edmundsen 1987).

It is important to stress again that both of these language assessments are standardized for home-language English speakers, and need to be used with caution with children new to English: the language age norms cannot be applied.

In the event, carrying out these brief assessments proved to be rather difficult. Child A did show that she knew more English than was expected based on her silence in the classroom, but she was extremely reluctant to answer any questions, or to repeat the story when shown the picture cues for the story assessment. She needed frequent prompts. She made little eye contact and spoke in an exceedingly quiet voice. The entire assessment was marked by extreme hesitation and long pauses on her part. She did however show a reasonable level of spoken English in the few replies she gave.

Child B was much more verbally forthcoming during the initial assessment, which came as a surprise considering how silent he was in the classroom. However he was reluctant to follow the test instructions, preferring to talk about his own interests, and the results of these formal assessments do not reflect his real gains in social communication. During the formal assessments, this child at times seemed not to be listening at all. In a speech and language therapy session a speech therapist would have addressed this in a very careful way, as listening is a crucial skill in learning language, but at that time it was necessary to get some measure of his spoken language ability and therefore the test had to be continued.

However it was remarkable how much he did speak, in English, during these initial formal assessments, and suddenly he was not the silent child of the classroom but a child with a lot to say, and a surprisingly wide vocabulary and grammatical competence in English. His silence in the classroom, it seemed, was not due to a lack of knowledge of English, but something very different. The StoryFrames programme thus turned out to be the very kind of programme he needed in order to become a confident communicative user of language in the classroom.

For this child, there was an added complication: a slight dysfluency (stuttering) when he spoke freely. This might very well have been a major factor in his silence at school, and goes to show yet again that a speech and language assessment of each child would be a very relevant thing to do, if this were feasible from a school's staffing and budget point of view. However, in spite of his dysfluency, after the programme this child was a very vocal child in the classroom and participated in group activities which required speaking. He also began to play with a range of children, which he had not done previously.

This all goes to show the complexity involved in language and communication in general, and how many factors might influence each and every child on a daily basis.

The pre-programme assessments presented therefore a rather confusing picture of the language levels of these two children. On one hand, their better-than-expected vocabulary and grammar provided evidence of the effectiveness of intensive language input: they had clearly been hearing and absorbing English during their months of silence. The inconclusive results of some of the formal assessments reinforces the important of using observational assessments of pragmatic language skills (the social use of language) in addition to using formal language assessments of vocabulary and grammar.

An additional and very pleasing knock-on effect of the intervention was the change which took place in the teaching practice of the staff at the school. Staff members came to listen in (unobtrusively) on some of the sessions, and asked for training courses on working with second-language and silent children. There were several informal discussions about other children who were causing concern. It may be therefore that ongoing frequent visits to individual children, with subsequent shared discussion with all the teachers over the course of the 6 weeks of the programme, can be a more effective way to initiate change in educational practice than one-off staff training sessions.

Assessment results for Child A

Child A showed a dramatic increase in vocabulary, grammar and sentence length by the end of the programme. On the teacher observation checklist, she showed excellent development in social skills and play: prior to the programme she did not play with other children at all, but by the end of the programme (10 weeks' duration) her social skills and play had advanced by the equivalent of about two years, and a few months later her social skills and play were above the level expected for her age group.

Informal discussions were held with the two teachers of Child A, three weeks after the intervention had ended. One of these teachers reported that Child A was for the first time initiating conversation with teachers. Both reported that she was now using a louder voice with both peers and teachers. She was also playing with other children and taking an active verbal role in the play.

The Teacher Observation evaluation which was used at the time of the original research is based on the table in Appendix III.

TEACHER OBSERVATION	NAME: CHILD A			
	Attention Age equivalent	Understanding Age equivalent	Speech & language Age equivalent	Social interaction & play Age equivalent
March 2009 Chronological age 4 yrs 5 months	3 yrs	3yrs	2yrs	2yrs
July 2009 Chronological age 4 yrs 9 months	4 yrs	3 yrs	3 yrs	4 yrs
October 2009 Chronological age 5 years	4 yrs	4 yrs	4 yrs	5 yrs

Assessment results for CHILD B

Child B, though silent in class, was voluble in the initial assessment. He talked loudly and at length, though somewhat dysfluently. He made little eye contact and showed little awareness of turn taking.

His key worker speculated that perhaps it was the opportunity to "hold the floor" and be listened to without competition from siblings or other children which led him to talk so freely during the sessions. Whatever the reason, it was felt that this child's real achievement would occur when he slowed down, spoke more calmly, and took into account that conversation involved two people and not one.

As observed by the class teacher, after the StoryFrames programme he showed significant progress in social interaction and play with peers, and he was showing social skills above his chronological age when observed several months after the programme had ended.

This child also made some progress in vocabulary and grammar. This was clearly evident during the StoryFrames sessions in the secluded space, but was not always matched by his vocabulary and grammar when speaking in the classroom.

In achieving the main aim of the StoryFrames programme, which was to bring the child to a place where he could interact, play and socialise comfortably with his peers and their teachers, this programme was successful.

For Child B, the initial positive changes reported by his mother and observed by me and by his teachers in the classroom seem to have diminished slightly at a re-test 5 months after the intervention period. He was reported by a teacher to have reverted to some extent to his previous dysfluency, as well as being sometimes "moody" and quiet for periods during the day. He did however continue to speak more than previously; he was no longer a 'silent child'; but he preferred to speak when fewer people are around.

It is likely that the very short duration of the intervention (6 weeks), in spite of the progress made, was insufficient for this child, and that he would have benefitted from a much longer intervention period in order to sustain his progress. He might also have benefitted from a more traditional speech and language therapy intervention.

For this child, therefore, the specific skill in the social use of language which was looked for by the end of the programme was allowing the teacher, or another child, to take a more equal number of conversational turns. This would include, for example, the child pausing in his speech for the other person to respond, or listening to the other person and responding contingently.

This is not to say that his turn-taking did not progress: improvement was noted on several occasions by the class teacher. But it was felt that more work on this aspect was needed for this child.

The skills in the social use of language which did progress well for Child B, and were still maintained several months after the end of the programme, were:

- Asking for information
- Answering the teacher's questions
- Expressing opinions or suggesting something new or different
- Verbal pretend play and collaborative dialogue with other children
- Joining in with the play of other children in the playground.

TEACHER OBSERVATION	NAME: CHILD B			
	Attention Age equivalent	Understanding Age equivalent	Speech & language Age equivalent	Social interaction & play Age equivalent
March 09 Chronological age 3 yrs 8 months 11 days	3years	3yrs	3yrs	3yrs
July 09 Chronological age 4 years	3yrs	3yrs	3yrs	4yrs
October 09 Chronological age 4 years 3 months	4yrs	3yrs	3yrs	5yrs

APPENDIX III

The development of language and communication skills

The following table provides a quick reference to stages of development for children learning a first language. These stages are most likely to be very different for children learning a second or third language: these children might reach each stage somewhat later, and may not necessarily follow the order of the stages as set out in the table below.

The table is presented merely as a guide in order to become familiar with the four aspects of language development which were used in the original research programme for the teacher evaluations before and after the programme: Listening and attention, understanding of language, speech and talk, and social skills and play.

This table cannot be used as a prescriptive sequence of development for children learning additional languages.

	Listening & Attention	Understanding of Language	Speech & Talk	Social Skills & Play
6 months	Looking carefully at faces Attends fleetingly to new objects, actions and events Quietens to listen to the speech of others	Recognises familiar voices and sounds and looks towards them	Expresses self with facial expressions, babbling, cries and vocal sounds & body movements Attempting to copy others facial expressions and sounds, like "oo" & "ar"	Explores objects by putting them in his/her mouth Reaches for objects and enjoys shaking objects Smiles and laughs
12 months	Attends to highly motivating objects with stimulating lights, sounds, different textures and colours Easily distracted from what he/she is looking at and doing	Understands familiar words and phrases like "No", "Bye", "Where's mum?" & "Want milk" Looks when own name is called Following simple directions when gesture is added e.g. "Give me the ball" & "Where are your shoes?"	Starts using a few a few single words like "mum", "dad" & "car" Babbles frequently and in long strings Copies simple speech sounds when face to face with a familiar teacher	Uses lots of gestures (e.g. pointing, waving, clapping) and facial expressions to express self Enjoys social games like peek-a-boo with a familiar teachers Offers toys to teacher as a way of interacting socially Uses familiar objects appropriately e.g. brushes hair, puts spoon to mouth
18 months	Attends to communication if it is clearly directed to him/her Focuses on an activity of own choice but can be easily distracted Interested in familiar songs and music	Understands simple instructions like "Give me the cup" without any clues Points to some body parts when asked e.g. "Where's your nose?" Points out familiar people and objects when asked e.g. "Where's the car", "Where's Grandma?"	Uses at least 10 single words, sometimes in combination with babble Sometimes copies words used by familiar teachers Combines a gesture with a word e.g. points and says 'car', waves and says 'bye'	Enjoys having an impact on the world around them e.g. dropping toys, pushing buttons to make a sounds or make lights flash Prefers to be with a familiar teacher than to play alone and will watch them closely, often copying things they do
2 years	Focuses on an activity he/she likes but finds it difficult if the teacher directs too much Concentrates for familiar songs and rhymes and tries to join in	Understands many everyday words (200 at least) Follows simple two part directions without any clues e.g. "Go to your room and get your shoes"	Can use around 50 words Says phrases or asks questions with two or three words together e.g. "My ball", "Big car", "Want biscuit", "Where's my drink?" Pronounces vowels sounds and early consonants, such as 'b', 'p', 'm', 'd', 'n', 'h'	Shows use of pretend play e.g. puts dolly to bed, feeds food to pretend animals Frustrated when not understood by teachers Will play alone sometimes but likes a familiar teacher to be close by

Age	Attention & Listening	Understanding	Talking	Play & Social
3 years	Focuses intently on activities but can still be easily distracted by other exciting things happening close by	Understands concepts words e.g. "Get a big one", "It goes under the table" Understands questions like "What's your name?", "Who's hiding in there?", "Where are we going?" Understand a short story with pictures	Asks questions Uses short sentences with around 4 – 5 words, like "daddy driving the car", "Want milk please mum", "Sing the bus song" May stumble over his/her words when forming new sentences Speech is usually easily understood but some consonants sounds like 'l', 'r', 'f', 'v', 's', 'z', 'sh', 'ch', 'j' & 'th' may still be difficult to say in words	Shows a full sequence in pretend play e.g. cooking dinner, feeding dolly and then putting dolly to bed Plays meaningfully with toys and talks to commentate on what's happening Engages in short conversation just sometimes jumps from one topic to another very quickly
4 years	Can attend to activities for long periods of time but will need to stop to fully listen to what a speaker is saying	Understanding instructions with three or more unrelated parts e.g. "Get a book, stand by the door and put your hands on your head" Understands 'why' questions e.g. "Why is he crying?" Understands some abstract ideas like 'yesterday', 'before', 'tomorrow'	Uses sentences often with up to 6 words or more e.g. "I want to play with cars", "Where did my ball go?", "I am making a funny one with big eyes" Asks lots of questions about various topics Able to remember and enjoys telling simple stories and singing songs When speaking in sentences speech is easily understood by a wide range of people but still finds the 'r', 'ch', 'j', 'sh' and 'th' sounds difficult to say in words	Enjoys playing with peers and will argue if things don't go smoothly Holds conversations, understands turn taking and sharing Shows complex role play and uses imagination to come up with new ideas
5 years	Able to listen to a speaker whilst staying focused on a task	Understands complex instructions with words like 'first', 'then' and 'last' Understand jokes and humour Follows a story without pictures Understands and enjoys rhyme	Sentences with about eight words (and sometimes more) e.g. "We went shopping and I got sweeties" Can re-tell a sequence of events or short story Asks what unfamiliar words mean May find the 'th' & 'r' consonants sounds difficult to produce in words and three consonant blends may still be tricky e.g. 'scr' or 'str'	Chooses who to play with and usually plays cooperatively Negotiates with peers how a play activity will happen

APPENDIX IV

Expanding high-level conversations

This appendix provides ideas for further expanding a child's communication.

This level of communication is not something one would expect, or aim for, in the initial stages of work with a silent child; the level of language being used here is complex and abstract. The level of free conversation presented in this section is not one of the explicit aims of the StoryFrames programme; the aim of the programme is to get to an adequate level of social interaction where the child emerges from their silence and takes an active part in the general interaction in the classroom.

However in some cases, when a child has emerged from silence, we find that their language levels turn out to be more advanced than we might have expected. For such children, further experience in using language in more advanced conversations would be beneficial.

Occasionally, after a number of sessions during which we have followed the F, R, A, M, and E stages, the child might begin to chat freely with the teacher, without using the toys at all. Sometimes, after we have read a picture book to the child, the child comments on an event in the book, or asks a question, or is reminded by the book about something similar from their own life.

This can occur once we have reached the Expanding stage of the programme. It is a time when free conversation between the teacher and the child might be possible, and desirable, if there are time and resources available. And of course, if the child initiates this kind of high-level discussion and conversation in a session, we pick up on it and run with it.

The spiral diagram above represents how such a conversation might proceed. It starts (in the middle of the spiral) with one person saying something, or pointing to something (joint attention) and from there the conversation develops continually, without a definite stopping point. The meandering nature of such conversation is similar to the dialogue of two friends having a chat over a cup of coffee, or when two children are just idly chatting about whatever interests them at any moment.

There are no set topics, and no required grammatical constructions; it is just a free and spontaneous conversation. At any stage, one of the participants in the conversation can add an idea, and the conversation might start a new spiral, or curl back to the original one. Or the conversation may come to its natural end.

In this kind of dialogue, we do not need to stick to one topic, although that is an option if the participants wish to. Sometimes we talk about other related things (this is where the small spiral shapes go off in different directions) and then we are free to come back to the main point of our conversation - or go off on another tangent. As long as the conversation keeps going, we let it run along its own trajectory.

The teacher tries to make sure that both partners (teacher and child) have at least the same amount of time, or the same number of turns, to talk; we try not to talk more than the child does. If however the child does talk more than we do, that is all to the good: we are giving a previously silent child a chance to express ideas, thoughts and feelings.

The main idea however is that two people are having a conversation together, and the child is not a passive listener but an active partner in a spiralling conversation.

How to deal with questions in free conversation

The teacher's task is not to ask too many questions, but rather to try to elicit questions from the child. In order to keep the conversation flowing, if we do ask a question, and the child answers, our job is *to respond to the child's answers.* We make sure that *every answer starts a new discussion*: the child's answer is the start of a discussion, not the end of the discussion.

In order to keep the conversation flowing, without explicitly asking too many questions, a useful technique is "pondering": for example, "I wonder what it would be like if..." "I wonder how that felt...". In this way we can suggest some quite abstract and even philosophical ideas, without making the child feel that they are being put on a spot and have to answer our questions.

Try to let the child have the last word!

Practicing this strategy

Look at the opening sentences below. What would you (Teacher = T) say next? What might the child (C) answer? What could you say next to keep the conversation going for more and more turns?

Examples

> Child says: "I can't find my shoe!!"
> T:
> C:
> T:
> C:
> C:

| Child says: "The doggie got lost!" |
| T: |
| C: |
| T: |
| C: |
| C: |

| Child says: "I'm finished painting my picture." |
| T: |
| C: |
| T: |
| C: |
| C: |

| Teacher says: who is not in class today? |
| C: Eddie! |
| T: |
| C: |
| T: |
| C: |
| C: |

| T says: what did we do outside last week? |
| C: Bubbles! |
| T: |
| C: |
| T: |
| C: |
| C: |

APPENDIX V

The miniature hand-made books of the Bronte family

The Brontës were a nineteenth-century literary family, born in the village of Thornton and later associated with the village of Haworth in the West Riding of Yorkshire, England. The sisters, Charlotte (1816–1855), Emily (1818–1848) and Anne (1820–1849) are all, to this day, well-known poets and novelists. Like many contemporary female writers, they published their poems and novels under male pseudonyms: Currer, Ellis and Acton Bell. Their stories attracted attention for their passion and originality.

Charlotte's *Jane Eyre* was the first to find success, while Emily's *Wuthering Heights*, Anne's *The Tenant of Wildfell Hall* and other works were accepted as masterpieces of literature later.

The three sisters and their brother Branwell (1817–1848), were very close. As children, they developed their imaginations first through oral storytelling and play, set in an intricate imaginary world, and then through the collaborative writing of increasingly complex stories set in their fictional world. The deaths of their mother and two older sisters marked them and influenced their writing profoundly, as did their isolated upbringing.

The Brontë birthplace in Thornton is a place of pilgrimage and their later home, the parsonage at Haworth in Yorkshire, now the Brontë Parsonage Museum, has hundreds of thousands of visitors each year.

Charlotte and her brother Branwell made some miniature books after Branwell was given a set of miniature toy soldiers by his father. These 'little books', only a few centimetres in size, were hand-made by Charlotte, Emily and Anne. They consist of paper scraps sewn into covers made from everyday items such as sugar bags and wallpaper. In them the sisters created imaginary worlds.

*Ref: Wikipedia, https://en.wikipedia.org/wiki/Bront%C3%AB_family. Accessed 24.2.2023

AUTHOR BIOGRAPHY

Cynthia Pelman is a speech and language therapist. She has worked in this field for over 40 years, working mainly with young children presenting with speech, language or school learning challenges.

Cynthia has worked with children who have been diagnosed with Developmental Language Disability, phonological disability, dyspraxia, or dysarthria. She works with children who are on the Autistic Spectrum, consulting with parents and schools on how to help these children to achieve their potential.

She has also worked extensively with children who are reluctant to speak, whether due to Selective Mutism, or due to having to learn a second language after having moved from their home country. She has also worked with teenagers who are shy and quiet, who present as lacking in confidence to express their wishes and ideas.

Cynthia also works as consultant to women in various employment settings, promoting confident public speaking and assertiveness.

Cynthia has an M.Sc degree in Speech and Language Therapy (City University, London) and an M.A. degree in Teaching English as a Second Language (Institute of Education, University of London).

Cynthia was a founder member of the organisation Wordworks, which helps parents and teachers to develop effective programmes for language and literacy in young children in South Africa. https://www.wordsworks.org.za

Cynthia is a trained practitioner of the Instrumental Enrichment education method, which uses cognitive educational methods to promote learning, and which is especially helpful in developing the skills of people with learning difficulties. This method promotes the intrinsic motivation to learn, as well as helping students to develop insightful reasoning and cognitive efficiency.

https://www.icelp.info/home-3/about-us/instrumental-enrichment/

Cynthia has written two books about her work as a speech and language therapist. These are books of advocacy: they speak up for those who struggle to speak up for themselves. The books are based on real case studies, with names and places changed for confidentiality. She has also written a book about her work in South Africa, describing the challenges for a teacher in putting into practice the methods and philosophy of Instrumental Enrichment in a small, impoverished community.

For more information, please see her website www.cynthiapelman.com

Other books by Cynthia Pelman

Joshy Finds his Voice (2013)
The Voice of the Xenolith (2014)
Voices from the Sand (2015)

www.ingramcontent.com/pod-product-compliance
Lightning Source LLC
Chambersburg PA
CBHW042239180426
43198CB00043B/2987